"I first met Kent and Josephine in the Amazon. As you read this book, you will witness the exciting, challenging, fulfilling adventures in one of the most challenging areas of the world—the Amazon. It will keep your attention because they lived an amazing life, but they had a purpose that was above all purposes in the world, to serve the King of Kings in the depths of a jungle. Kent and Josephine are great missionaries, and this book will inspire you to be a missionary in the jungle of your life."

LOREN CUNNINGHAM
Founder, Youth With A Mission

"This is a page-turner. Set against the backdrop of the River People and the indigenous tribes of the Amazon rain forest, Kent and Josephine's story is more than an adventure, more than an inspiration; this is a guide to meaningful living for everybody. This book is full of profound insight; my wife and I could not put it down. From the first page we were transported into an exciting journey that captured our imagination completely. We shed tears, we cheered triumphs, we marveled at the courage, tenacity, humility, and love expressed through this family and their friends."

JOHN DAWSON
President emeritus, Youth With A Mission

"Kent and Josephine were wonderful partners in our YWAM Amazon years. Their book will give you a glimpse into their adventurous, sacrificing, and many times funny and joyful missionary family life. If you are considering a life in missions, married or not, this book is a must-read. If you want to understand a little more of the mechanics of cross-cultural relationships in a foreign land, you will learn precious lessons here."

BRÁULIA & REINALDO RIBEIRO
Founders of YWAM Porto Velho and former leaders of Tribal Ministries

"Kent and I grew up together in Minnesota; we lived on the same street, went to the same church and both joined Youth With A Mission, becoming full-time missionaries. Kent and Josephine formed a dynamic team. As a young couple they obeyed the call of God to go to Brazil to work among the remote river people of the Amazon. Kent and Josephine are authentic Christ followers—their commitment heroic, their faith vibrant, and their obedience unwavering. Their book is a modern-day adventure story that is a must read!"

SEAN LAMBERT
International founder, Homes of Hope; president, YWAM San Diego/Baja

"*River People* is a compelling mission adventure story about the extraordinary lengths God will go to reach unreached people groups through willing vessels, yet supplying grace, humor, and lavish provisions the whole journey. This concise yet exciting and informative narrative communicates the romance, cross-cultural hurdles, and steps of faith encountered in missional church-planting where none have ventured before. Recommended reading and great teaching material for novice long-term frontier mission training as well as faith-building for all believers."

DANIEL THOMAS, MD, PHD
The Gate International Church, San Francisco

"I could not put this book down! It is not only a true adventure but an inspiring road map for all who commit to obediently follow the Lord in the front line of missions. The kingdom principles forged in the fires of affliction will strengthen future generations as they follow in the path of these YWAM pioneers, and the keys given as to how to shift principalities over regions will further reward them."

JENNIFER HAGGER, AM
Founder and director, Australian House of Prayer for All Nations and Mission World Aid; senior pastor, Zion Hill Christian Community

"I met this couple as two single young people working in missions. I watched closely as they came together, raised an excellent family, and did a quality job improving wholistically the lives of people in a remote, primitive place. That proves again that serving needy people successfully in these kinds of environments can be done by people who are not preachers by trade, who are newly married, and who have their family on a boat in the jungle. This story should encourage and enthuse thousands of young people with what the possibilities are for them to bring lasting change to societies virtually anywhere in their world while still having good marriages, families, educations, strong relationship with God, and being fulfilled in line with their unique desires and callings."

DEAN SHERMAN
International lecturer, University of the Nations

"From the moment I opened *River People* I was drawn into the journey that Kent and Josephine embarked on. Every chapter was gripping; it was like reading a thriller novel, but this story was real! Young and old will love it and be inspired and challenged."

DIANA HALLAS
Youth With A Mission

"All nations are proud of their heroes; the church is also. Kent and Josephine marked, with deep footprints, a part of the church's history in one of the most difficult regions of the world, the Amazon region of Brazil. It is impossible to read their story and not glorify God."

ROBSON OLIVEIRA
Author and missionary to Africa and India; Youth With A Mission, Brazil

"What a joy to read this thrilling adventure! It's a story that needed to be told. What does it look like for a young couple to venture into the remote interior of Amazonia with their four children and faithfully serve a faithful God? Kent and Josephine wisely weave key missionary insights and strategies into their story, making it not only an exciting read but one that will instruct further generations of frontier missionaries."

TODD KUNKLER
VP marketing, Dreamline Aviation

"This book offers a compelling narrative, with vivid description of a family's life and ministry on the Amazon River. It is filled with practical advice to those who, like them, might be willing to give a significant portion of their lives on behalf of others."

DR. TODD JOHNSON
Associate professor, Gordon-Conwell Theological Seminary

"*River People* is both colorful and riveting. It personally challenged me. As I compared my experience to Kent and Josephine's, there were passages in which I felt like I was spiritually underdeveloped and was challenged to increase my reliance on God's loving direction and sovereignty. This is a must-read for those desiring what Oswald Chambers calls a life of 'spontaneous, joyful uncertainty and expectancy.'"

BOB MOFFITT
Author of If Jesus Were Mayor; *president, Harvest Foundation; cofounder, Disciple Nations Alliance*

"A beautiful girl from Down Under meets a Minnesota boy and together they end up bringing the Story of His grace and mercy to the heart of the Amazon jungle. Follow this amazing story, a weaving of God's making, full of unexpected twists and turns, and just try to put this superbly written book down as you read this marvelous account of His life lived out through two people and their family pursuing His glory in the nations. A beautiful testimony."

BRYAN THOMPSON
Europe Director, Simply the Story

"I highly recommend this book. It is an amazing story of a modern missionary family's struggles and victories as they bring hope to the peoples of the Amazon rain forest. It is raw, and it is real. I had the privilege of playing a small role in the beginning days of this adventure—an adventure that truly changed my life and helped to chart the course of what would become the incredible journey you are about to experience. It is rare to see the kind of dedication to God and the sacrifice for the needs of people that you will see demonstrated in this book. An attitude of 'Not my will; but Your will be done' is the theme that runs throughout every chapter and every story. Be prepared to be challenged by the simplicity of trust in God and the profound miracles that follow."

CALVIN CONKEY
Cofounder, Create International

"I have known and admired this amazing couple, Kent and Josephine, for many years. Reading this book will take you on an adventure with them into one of the most remote and challenging places on earth—the Amazon. Their willingness to follow God's call to work among those who have never heard about Jesus is inspirational. Every step of their journey as a married couple and as a family is a lesson in the simplicity of listening to God and obeying him. You will be challenged by their perseverance through many tests and trials, as they and their team pioneer a growing indigenous community of Jesus followers. They share some of the lessons learned in an honest and refreshing way, which makes great reading. So grateful to Kent and Josephine for writing this account for the next generation of pioneers."

DAVID COLE
Board of regents chairperson, University of the Nations, Singapore

"How far are you willing to go to see a dream come true, especially if you believe it is a dream from God? A family of six braves life in the wilds of the Amazon to do just that! I've had the honor of seeing—up close and personal— some of the results of their work. This hair-raising adventure will help you see it too. You'll be strengthened along the way with practical, faith-building truths. Our prayer is that you will follow this family's example: risking it all to bring more people into God's kingdom. There are still thousands of tribes and peoples who've never heard the Good News about Jesus. Let's help fulfill God's dream, that all will hear."

KEVIN & LAURA SUTTER
International leaders, YWAM Frontier Missions

RIVER PEOPLE

*Taking God's Love and Transforming
Power to the Amazon*

KENT AND JOSEPHINE TRUEHL

YWAM PUBLISHING
Seattle, Washington

YWAM Publishing is the publishing ministry of Youth With A Mission (YWAM), an international missionary organization of Christians from many denominations dedicated to presenting Jesus Christ to this generation. To this end, YWAM has focused its efforts in three main areas: (1) training and equipping believers for their part in fulfilling the Great Commission (Matthew 28:19), (2) personal evangelism, and (3) mercy ministry (medical and relief work).

For a free catalog of books and materials, call (425) 771-1153 or (800) 922-2143. Visit us online at www.ywampublishing.com.

River People: Taking God's Love and Transforming Power to the Amazon
Copyright © 2016 by Kent and Josephine Truehl

Published by YWAM Publishing
a ministry of Youth With A Mission
P.O. Box 55787, Seattle, WA 98155-0787

Library of Congress Cataloging-in-Publication Data is on file at the Library of Congress.

ISBN 978-1-57658-940-3 (paperback)
ISBN 978-1-57658-652-5 (e-book)

Unless otherwise noted, Scripture quotations in this book are taken from The Holy Bible, New International Version®, NIV® Copyright © 1973, 1978, 1984 by Biblica, Inc.® Used by permission. All rights reserved worldwide. Verses marked NASB are taken from the New American Standard Bible, © 1960, 1962, 1963, 1968, 1971, 1972, 1973, 1975, 1977 by The Lockman Foundation. Used by permission. Verses marked NKJV are taken from the New King James Version, Copyright © 1979, 1980, 1982 by Thomas Nelson, Inc., Publishers. Used by permission. Verses marked NRSV are from the New Revised Standard Version of the Bible, © 1989 by the Division of Christian Education of the National Council of Churches of Christ in the U.S.A. Used by permission. All rights reserved.

First printing 2016

Printed in the United States of America

To our four children and to our future generations.
Sasha Bethany, Chloe Christiana, Alexandra Victoria, and
Jonathan Christian—you shared this Amazon journey with
us. We see now that your unique childhood years, filled with
adventures and challenges, have formed you into the amazing
individuals you are today.

And to the River People of the Purus River and Lábrea,
Amazonas, who we lived among and who became lifelong
friends. This is your story too.

International Adventures

Adventures in Naked Faith

Against All Odds

Bring Your Eyes and See

A Cry from the Streets

Dayuma: Life Under Waorani Spears

Cell 58: Imprisoned in Iran

Living on the Devil's Doorstep

Love Notes to God

The Man with the Bird on His Head

The Narrow Road

Taking On Giants

Taking the High Places

Tomorrow You Die

Torches of Joy

Totally Surrounded

Walking Miracle

A Way Beyond Death

Contents

Authors' Note

A S a young married couple in missions training, we meditated on the Great Commission in Matthew 28:18–20, "Then Jesus came to them and said, 'All authority in heaven and on earth has been given to me. Therefore go and make disciples of all nations, baptizing them in the name of the Father and of the Son and of the Holy Spirit, and teaching them to obey everything I have commanded you. And surely I am with you always, to the very end of the age.'" We asked God for a ministry assignment that would suit our young family—a place where our children could learn another language and culture and be fully part of our calling in transforming communities with God's loving presence and salvation through community development based on Luke 2:52, "And Jesus grew in wisdom and stature, and in favor with God and men." Our focus was a holistic attempt to bring education, health care, and spiritual and social development to the areas where the community desired change. It was, and will always be, a deep privilege to co-labor with and serve such an amazing God. All glory and deep gratitude to Him for everything accomplished.

"'My grace is sufficient for you, for my power is made perfect in weakness.' Therefore I will boast all the more gladly about my weaknesses, so that Christ's power may rest on me" (2 Corinthians 12:9).

PART ONE

Rivers and Jungles

There the majestic LORD will be for us
A place of broad rivers and streams.
ISAIAH 33:21 (NKJV)

ONE

The First Kiss

SHE caught my attention from the first day of class. Besides being very good-looking, I found her full of energy, well organized, fast paced, and fun. I also found her care and love for people, her delightful disposition, and her resolute commitment to God and missions very attractive. We seemed a good match, yet the details of how "us" could possibly eventuate seemed too complex. For starters, I was American and she was Australian. To complicate matters further, her US visa expired, resulting in a move to Hong Kong, while I remained in Los Angeles.

After sixteen months she was back in LA for the summer, but the long-distance relationship thing had left us uncertain. She was with a team from Hong Kong ministering to Chinese in West LA before going to Brazil for even more outreach. I was organizing transportation and food for 660 outreach participants east of Los Angeles. Our full schedules, and living on opposite sides of the sprawling megacity, made it almost impossible to find time together. However, I think we both knew that it was now or never as far as "us" was concerned, so we finally stole away an entire evening.

Josephine was a romantic. Unfortunately I was too broke and too busy for romance, so our date was a simple picnic in a small, grassy park. It was a hot July evening. Soon the park filled and became so busy that for a chance at a more intimate conversation we were forced to retreat back into the stuffy old car I had borrowed. For three hours we discussed topic after topic in a gradual progression toward the question of "us." Although tentative and apprehensive, we both decided to open up, knowing that only one thing really mattered—do we love each other?

For the next two hours we felt like actors in our own movie, as if having an out-of-body experience and watching ourselves from above. Gradually the realization of genuine love settled safely in our hearts. As it did, complexity fell away. We spoke of marriage and children. Around midnight I drove Josephine home and walked her to the door. We shared our first kiss.

Josephine returned from outreach in Brazil just days before Christmas. Together we flew to Hong Kong, where we collected her belongings, had our wedding rings made, and bought satin fabric and lace. Josephine, ceaselessly thrifty and creative, was going to make her wedding dress.

Finally we arrived in Australia. The Sydney Harbour Bridge and Opera House were more stunning in reality than what I had seen on TV. Josephine was excited to share her country with me, so we traveled overland to South Australia for a more personal experience of the place and its people.

It was summer in the land down under. Huge white cockatoos and gray and pink galahs screeched so loudly you could hear them through the thick windows of the bus, even with the air-conditioning blasting. As dusk fell, kangaroos appeared silently, grazing peacefully near the road's edge, then bounded away effortlessly as the economy coach raced past. The sun sank into the desert continent with heat shimmering like rolling silver waves on the distant horizon. The sunburned land was a polar opposite of the punishing cold of the Minnesota winters I grew up in. This was the first time my winter had turned to summer, but it was not just any summer. I was getting married.

Brazil

THE plane soared south over the South American rainforest, a jungle larger than all other jungles of the world put together. In the two hours since sunrise I'd seen nothing below but a vast sea of green, a tropical forest canopy hiding three lands you seldom hear about: Guyana, French Guiana, and Suriname. Only winding rivers of creamy brown or dark coffee colors broke the seemingly endless leafy expanse. They looked so different from the blue rivers of Minnesota. In the Sioux Indian language, *Minnesota* means "land of sky-blue waters." This morning my mind kept comparing the rivers below with North America's largest river, the mighty Mississippi, which flowed just a mile from my childhood home in suburban Minneapolis. On warm days, I rode my bicycle there with the other boys to fish, play, swim, and rope swing. The Mississippi seemed so enormous to me then, almost one thousand feet wide. That experience had defined my concept of a great river—until today.

The rivers, lakes, and forests of Minnesota constitute a huge wilderness of water and woods. I loved those woods. I had a sense that I would love this great forest too.

The FASTEN YOUR SEATBELTS sign illuminated with a loud *pong*, then the pilot rattled off a bunch of instructions in Portuguese.

"We are beginning our descent," the pilot then said in heavily accented English. "We are 167 kilometers from our destination."

Belém, Brazil, was our destination, the largest city of the Amazon jungle, located about eighty miles from the Atlantic and the mouth of the Amazon River.

"We are, at this very moment, flying over the equator," the pilot added.

Along with everyone else in a window seat, I looked out the airplane window for a line marking the middle of the world. Again, I saw only green, except for another river that looked like a squiggly length of yarn thrown across an inconceivably huge grassy lawn—just one of the Amazon's eleven hundred tributaries. I followed its meander through the emerald forest into the distance.

Then I saw it. A loud "Wow!" burst out of my mouth at the sight of the Amazon River. It was like a giant beige carpet runner leading through a majestic cathedral of green. It was a hundred times wider than the tributaries that fed it. I remained mesmerized as we flew over. All eyes gazed out the airliner's windows in fascination. Tiny wooden boats hugged the edge, as if in fear of venturing across the turbulent expanse.

I glanced at my two traveling companions from the Youth With A Mission (YWAM) training center in Los Angeles. I could see excitement rising in their sleep-deprived faces. The three of us were embarking on an adventure we could never have imagined when we started working together two years earlier.

Then I saw it again! How could this be . . . another Amazon River? But there it was, an immense milky brown, mega-expressway stampeding straight through the jungle toward the rising sun. Our flight path from Miami to Belém was bringing us over the estuary, where the mighty river splits into channels around Marajó, an island the size of Switzerland. What I saw first must have been the Amazon's northernmost channel; now I was seeing the second channel.

We flew over another stretch of jungle on Marajó, laced with little rivers and channels that looked like a biology textbook sketch of arteries, veins, and capillaries. After fifteen minutes I saw another huge body of water that I thought was the Atlantic Ocean, but the pilot called it the Pará River, explaining it was the southernmost channel of the Amazon. My mind could not take in the size. The Mississippi River I was so impressed with as a child was trivial by comparison. Doing a quick calculation as we descended, I computed that the one-thousand-foot-wide Mississippi near my home was less than a quarter mile wide, compared with the mouth of the main channel of the Amazon, which is nine miles wide. And the whole Amazon estuary is 202 miles wide. My jaw dropped.

Our arrival in Belém brought more surprises: humidity that soaked you and choked you at the same time, and a racially diverse population. I had always thought of Brazilians as brown-skinned Latinos, but here were Japanese, native Indians, and Europeans. I was most surprised by the large number of African Brazilians. My Brazil travel book said the number of slaves transported to the country between 1525 and 1866 was ten times the number brought into the United States. Gerson Ribeiro, the founder of YWAM Amazon, was African Brazilian. He met us the moment we exited immigration and customs. He stood over six feet tall and flashed a wide smile. He was handsomely dressed and looking happy.

"Welcome to Brazil!" He stretched out his hand to each of us—first to Todd Kunkler, a theologian type and leader of our missions program in LA, then to Calvin Conkey, a humorous sidekick and missionary anthropologist, and then to me.

"My name is Kent—Kent Truehl," I said, acting as confident as possible.

We piled our gear into a taxi and headed for YWAM Belém. There we met the assistant director, Alcír, and a young woman who introduced herself with about four names. The Portuguese sounds were so new I could only remember her first name, Bráulia. She was young and pretty and fit my stereotypical image of a Brazilian, with tan skin and a head of dark brown curls.

Gerson explained they had a lot to do before tomorrow's departure, so he commissioned a girl named Anabel to be our tour guide for the day. She looked about fifteen years old, but Gerson said she was one of the four women on YWAM's first team to work with a tribal group, so I guessed she was older than she looked.

As we waited for a bus to town, the never boring Calvin went straight to the point and asked Anabel how old she was.

"I'm twenty-one, the same age as Bráulia."

"Can you help me learn Portuguese?"

"Only if you help me in my English," she said slowly.

"Not *in* my English . . . *with* my English," Calvin corrected.

"*With* my English," Anabel repeated carefully.

We got on a bus that was nearly empty, but it quickly filled until people were standing in the aisle, including a woman near Calvin. He wanted to offer his seat to her so he asked Anabel, "How do I say *woman* in Portuguese?"

Anabel told him the word quietly.

"*Mule-hair?*" Calvin blurted in his attempt to imitate Anabel. Calvin has a booming voice, so everybody looked at him.

"No. *Mu-lh-er.*" Anabel pronounced it slowly for Calvin. She enlightened the three of us that the Portuguese *lh* combination doesn't exist in English, and therefore is difficult for Americans.

"*Mool-yh-er, Mool-yher, Moolyheir,*" Calvin practiced out loud, intent on proving Anabel wrong. The woman standing next to Calvin started backing away from this large, bearded gringo who sat alone repeating *woman, woman, woman.*

Once off the bus, we feverishly followed Anabel through the crowded sidewalks of downtown, like ducklings behind their mother duck. She walked quickly and with purpose, taking us to a money changer. We lost sight of her momentarily as she exited the sidewalk into a fabric shop. We stopped at the entrance, assuming it was a shopping detour. Anabel kept walking her furious pace right to the front and was visibly annoyed when she saw us still standing on the sidewalk. She raised her arms in the unmistakable "What the?" gesture.

As we hurried through the shop, I said to Calvin, "I guess when you're in another country—don't assume anything."

"You got that right," Calvin said as we climbed up a creaky wooden stairway.

Under the rafters above the shop, we saw a man sitting behind a wooden desk at the entrance to a small room. As he stood up, beads of sweat rolled down his large belly, which protruded from his unbuttoned shirt. There was a gun on top of the desk. We stopped. He acknowledged our submission by blowing cigarette smoke into our faces. As he poked his head inside the room to speak with someone, we did the "What the?" gesture to Anabel. The bouncer motioned us into the office.

"How much money do you want to exchange?" Anabel asked.

The three of us fumbled for our wallets and simultaneously pulled out a fifty each. As we handed our money to Anabel, Calvin whispered under his breath, "Is this legal?"

Todd, like a ventriloquist with a perfect smile plastered on his face, whispered back, "When in Rome, do as the Romans."

The money changer held up each bill to a light bulb, hanging by bare wires, to verify their authenticity. Then he punched his calculator and showed it to Anabel.

"*Ta bom,*" she said.

I assumed the two words were affirmative because the money changer pulled out an enormous stack of Brazilian bills and counted out a large pile for each of us.

We were done—down the stairs, through the shop, and out the door. Outside, we burst into a string of *Godfather* jokes that even got a smile out of Anabel. What a remarkable introduction to Brazil.

THREE

Itinerary of Adventure

WE spent the rest of the afternoon touring Belém—the City of Mango Trees. We were standing among mounds of stinking fish in a market when a monsoonal downpour began. It battered the tin roof so hard we couldn't hear a thing. We passed time gazing at tables laden with everything from prehistoric-looking fish to a huge freshwater specimen that breathed air and had scales the size of potato chips. I saw the small orange-bellied piranha with its fearsome razor-sharp teeth. The fish smell, together with jet lag and the tropical heat, made me queasy, so I grabbed a Coca-Cola from a refrigerated cabinet and sat down. Anabel returned my Coke to the cabinet, insisting we buy *guaraná* instead.

"What is guaraná?"

Anabel looked offended. "It's Brazil's most popular beverage! Far better than Coke."

The guy behind the counter poured us four glasses. Todd raised his glass in a toast and said, "To the Amazon."

"To the Amazon," we replied. Then in unison we gulped guaraná for the very first time.

"Ooh, that's good," Calvin said.

It was more than just good. Like most soft drinks, it was fizzy and sweet. But unlike anything else, guaraná combines a sugary apple-juice flavor with a nutty tang that leaves your throat raspy and your mouth debating if it was sweet or savory.

After more questions from Calvin, Anabel revealed with obvious pride that Belém, as well as her native Manaus, were the most prosperous cities in Brazil during the Amazon rubber boom from 1850 to 1920. We ended our tour with a walk down a boulevard lined with mango trees to a busy street where Anabel squeezed us into a crowded rush-hour bus and ordered us to hurry down the aisle.

"How do you say *excuse me*," I asked politely.

"You don't. You just push."

With that, she shoved the three of us through the crush of sweaty bodies. Two stops later she pushed us out the exit door onto the shoulder of the road. We huddled on a gravel island surrounded by enormous puddles of rainwater as the bus chugged away, belching a plume of diesel smoke over us. Anabel then navigated us into a large open-air restaurant to await the others.

Two bottles of guaraná later, Gerson, Alcír, and Bráulia arrived—they were an hour and a half late. Alcír and Gerson gave us firm handshakes, while I noticed Anabel and Bráulia greeted with three kisses. Actually, they seemed to just brush cheeks while kissing the air. When Bráulia came to me, I wasn't sure what to do, a handshake or three kisses. She smiled as she took my hand in a handshake but then also moved up close for a cheek kiss. I hurried to do the three kisses thing, but she moved away after the first, leaving me puckering in midair.

"You only get one kiss," Gerson said, then laughed loudly at my expense.

Todd came over and explained, "Single women three kisses, married women two kisses, but a man giving a woman a kiss, kisses only one cheek."

"I guess I missed that in the travel guide."

Gerson came across as authoritative and professional, with elements of a comic and a charmer mixed in. He and Alcír, in spite of the heat, were wearing beautifully pressed long-sleeve shirts. Anabel suddenly reappeared in a nice dress like Bráulia. All were fashionably dressed, while the three of us Americans in our jeans and T-shirts looked sloppy by comparison.

Todd, Calvin, and I then experienced Brazilian *churrasco* for the first time. This variation of barbecue involves putting large slabs of meat on long, knifelike skewers to cook slowly over wood charcoal. After the heat and smoke barbecues the meat to perfection, it is brought to your table, still on the long skewer. A waiter carves fine slices of the cooked outer layer onto your plate—as much as you want! The nonstop offering of a dozen cuts of meat was complemented by a buffet of rice, salads, salsa, fruits, and desserts. We ate until we could eat no more.

Jet-lagged, tired, and overfull, I could only sit and reflect on how different everything was—the river, the city, the food—but especially the people. These friends I was sitting with (but couldn't even speak to) were partners in the ministry that Josephine and I had already committed to. In order to make sense of my situation, I reviewed the events that got me here.

Our team in LA wanted to reach unreached people groups. Belém was one of the first Youth With A Mission locations to intentionally target unreached peoples—Amazon tribes. Todd—brother-in-law to John Dawson, the founder of YWAM Los Angeles—had insisted I join him and Calvin in a scouting trip to the Amazon. Josephine and I had seen no need for an advance trip, since a partnership between YWAM Los Angeles and YWAM Amazon had already been agreed to. Yet God spoke so clearly, and provided so miraculously, that I couldn't deny God's intentions for me to be here.

The waiter interrupted my reflection by taking my plate and motioning me to the dessert buffet. Because it was included in the price, everyone attempted to eat more, yet our metabolism and conversation soon ground to a halt. Gerson must have resolved that this lull in the evening was a good time to present the itinerary.

"Today is day one," he announced like a news broadcaster. "Tomorrow—day two—we fly to Manaus to do shopping. Day three we load supplies on the YWAM boat and leave Manaus. Then it will be three more days' travel to the town of Tapauá on the Purus River, the ministry location of Alcír and his team."

Alcír flashed a smile and waved, which triggered the Brazilians to start talking loudly, and all at once. It seemed rude to me, but Gerson didn't seem to mind and just continued.

"After Tapauá it will be three more days travel until we," pointing out Bráulia and the three of us with an exaggerated glance, "will hike in to a primitive tribal group."

"Awesome!" Calvin exclaimed like a child on Christmas morning. Visiting a primitive tribe was a dream come true for Calvin, who had just started his degree in applied missionary anthropology.

"It will be one day hiking in, one day in the tribe, then one day hiking out. Finally, it will be five days nonstop back to Manaus."

Everyone started talking all at once again while I experienced a peculiar combination of excitement and fear. Unlike Calvin, I had never studied anthropology or dreamed of going to a tribe, but it certainly energized me out of my food-induced stupor.

What would it be like to visit a primitive tribe? I was an inexperienced twenty-something, only just learning what it meant to be a missionary. Was I up to it?

I had no idea. Nevertheless, my heart was pounding at the thought of it.

FOUR

The Jungle Capital

THE Amazon rain forest is about two-thirds the area of America's forty-eight contiguous states, a fact I couldn't believe until we flew inland to Manaus, over nothing but jungle for nine hundred miles, and we weren't even halfway across. Bráulia said the tribe we were going to visit was just 119 people. I was beginning to understand how such a small tribe could remain unfound under that dark canopy of trees.

As we descended into Manaus, the capital of the Brazilian state of Amazonas, I was surprised by how large the city was, over one million people in the middle of the largest jungle on earth. Gerson hailed a taxi and checked us into the multistory Monaco Hotel.

"This is why we need a YWAM base in Manaus," Gerson said. "We can't afford a hotel every time we come here."

From the hotel's rooftop garden we looked over downtown and the Renaissance-style Opera House. It boasted steel walls from Scotland, bricks from Europe, French glass, Italian marble, and a domed roof of thirty-six thousand ceramic tiles painted in the colors of the national flag of Brazil. Amazing really, considering that the building was completed here, in the middle of the Amazon, back in 1896. Besides such interesting facts, Gerson answered our bombardment of questions about Manaus's importance as the geographic center of the jungle.

"We need a permanent location," he said. "My vision for YWAM Manaus is a property on the river to moor our boat, and God willing, the many boats we will have in the future."

Todd, Calvin, and I could see that boats made sense here, as the riverboats are the cars, campers, buses, and trucks of the region. Boats are a necessity, not an option, when ministering in the Amazon.

The next morning Gerson guided us to the old port of the city. It sat behind a thriving market, an impressive building whose steel structures were designed and built in France by Gustav Eiffel, of Eiffel Tower fame. The port housed boats of every description, from tiny to huge, and old to new—hundreds of them. Some empty, others packed to overflowing, some were freighters while others were passenger vessels—most looked like a combination of all of the above.

Gerson found the YWAM riverboat triple-parked behind other boats tied to the waterfront wall. The registered name painted on the hull was *São Mateus Singapura*, honoring St. Matthew's Lutheran Church in Singapore, which had donated money for its purchase. From where we stood on the wharf, I could see that the boat had a split-level design. The wheelhouse and a small cabin sat prominently at the top front of the boat, with a big room below, where hammocks were drooping.

I had figured out that there would be two teams on board. Gerson, Bráulia, Todd, Calvin, and I were the team of five hiking in to the tribe. Alcír was the leader of a team of two guys and two girls going to Tapauá, where a retiring missionary had recently handed over a church and a house to YWAM to continue the work.

I boarded first, suitcase in hand, and shuffled along the outer edge of a boat tied to the wharf. When I reached the stern, the wake of a big boat that had passed by out in the open water was now severely bobbing all boats in a very unequal unison. Two smiling deckhands motioned for me to climb through a large window into a big room under the wheelhouse of the YWAM riverboat. The others followed, carrying their personal belongings and contorting themselves through the window. We left our things in the open room, which looked just big enough for seven men in hammocks, and then walked upstairs.

"Welcome to our home," Joe and Marjory said with hands extended. Joe was introduced as the captain of the *São Mateus*. After meeting this retired American couple, we were introduced to the two smiling deck-hands who were now standing against the railing, overlooking the other boats and the hive of activity at the port.

"Edilberto," he said, pointing to himself with one hand while extending the other for a handshake.

"My name is Baia," the second guy said. "I spell for you, B-A-I-A, By-ee-ah."

"Thank you, Baia. Nice to meet you," I said as I shook his hand.

"I know your wife, Josephine," Baia said. "She came to my home-town of São Paulo with an evangelism team from Hong Kong that I translated for. We saw many people come to Christ through her team. We even came here to Manaus. She encouraged me to join YWAM. So here I am—a missionary in the Amazon!"

"That's awesome," I said. "Really nice to meet you, Baia."

He explained that he had just completed the Discipleship Training School, known as DTS in YWAM. He and Edilberto came along to drive the boat at night so we could travel 24/7. As we continued our chat, I saw a group of American tourists walking through the crowded port. They were sunburned and draped with gear. Captain Joe yelled out, "Here we are!" and waved his arms to get their attention.

"They're a short-term missions team coming with us," Gerson revealed. As fast as I could wonder *How many are there?* Gerson contin-ued, "They are a team of seven girls and three guys who will help Alcír build chicken coops, paint a church, paint a house, and do outreach."

I was doubtful fourteen people would fit on the *São Mateus*, but twenty-four was unquestionably too many. With those ten Americans plus Alcír and his team, the big open room was now small and claus-trophobic. Hammocks, suitcases, and numerous boxes of gear and sup-plies covered every inch of floor. The room was now packed wall to wall and floor to ceiling.

Gerson gave the three of us from LA a tiny cabin at the back of the boat that had one bunk bed so small Todd described it as a double-decker park bench. Two boxes of baby chickens, twenty-five per box, were also part of the cargo. I guessed they were the reason chicken coops needed to be built in Tapauá. There was no suitable place out of the wind for the baby chicks, except the tiny cabin. Todd had his stuff on the top bunk, so the chicks got put on the bottom bunk, which was my bunk. I took the thin foam mattress from underneath the baby chicks and decided to join Calvin, who had marked out a spot to sleep with his air mattress in the open-air on the metal sundeck above the galley. It was mid-August. They said it does not rain during the dry season months of July, August, and September. Calvin and I hoped that was true.

After two large blocks of ice and a huge box of fresh meat was delivered, the engine roared to life. The noise in the galley, its floor immediately above the engine, was deafening, and everything on the shelves rattled violently. The super excited American team ran to the top deck as we headed into open water. To take pictures everyone suddenly shifted to the same side, causing the boat to lean dangerously. Captain Joe burst out of the wheelhouse yelling, "Get away from the side or you'll tip us over!"

In spite of Captain Joe's stern warning, the same thing happened a half hour later when we reached the meeting of the waters. Here the black, warm water of the Negro River pours into the cooler, milky-colored water of the Solimões River. For nearly four miles these two mighty rivers join, but do not mix. When they do merge, they form the super-sized Amazon River for its final thousand-mile charge to the Atlantic.

I was so surprised when a pod of gray dolphins suddenly surfaced near the boat. I didn't know freshwater dolphins existed. Everyone was even more astonished to see two rare pink dolphins. Gerson said the dolphins come to hunt at the meeting of the waters, where the fish, confused by the sudden collision of density, temperature, and color, make easy prey.

Nightfall brought calm on deck and stability to the boat, but not much peace, as the engine maintained its deafening roar. Dinner emerged about 9:00 p.m. It was basic Brazilian—pleasantly flavored brown beans over rice with a few shreds of meat mixed in, and a side of canned corn. I also got a small serving of Coke in an old tomato paste jar.

The cool, damp night on the open river caused three chicks to die. The next morning a light bulb was connected in the cabin over the chicks to keep them warm. The light served its purpose and prevented chick deaths, but with the incessant chirping and the light on all night, Todd was having difficulty sleeping. The tiny cabin smelled like a pet store on the first day, a barnyard on the second, and a feedlot by the third. For three days running, from what I could gather, Calvin and I slept better than anyone—well, certainly better than Todd.

FIVE

Change in Plans

AFTER twenty-four hours going west up the Amazon River, our boat turned south onto the Purus River. The Indian tribe we were going to was about four hundred miles from Manaus in a straight line on the map. But since the Purus was full of curves and meanders, our actual traveling distance was about seven hundred miles, or as the Brazilians calculated, eleven hundred kilometers.

Captain Joe drove uncomfortably close to the riverbank. It made the jungle look like a towering wall on one side. The constant roar of the engine gave the sensation of speed, but when we came to a village, the waving children ran past on land faster than we were moving upriver.

I decided to go to the wheelhouse. Captain Joe was seated on a comfy elevated seat behind a panel of engine gauges, a depth finder, and a classic wooden ship wheel. To start a conversation, I inquired why we traveled so close to the edge.

"The current is less strong at the edge when going upriver," he replied.

"What gear are we in?" I asked, hoping we could go faster.

He replied, "Full speed ahead."

Captain Joe explained that there was only forward and reverse and that full speed ahead was about five miles per hour when going upstream. The thought of going five miles an hour for seven hundred miles robbed me of my cheerfulness. I could jog faster than the boat was moving. But then I rationalized that I couldn't jog 24/7 for seven days straight, so that made me feel better.

"The rivers are past flood stage and receding fast," Captain Joe continued, "so we can't cut any miles off the journey by taking shortcuts through the jungle."

"Shortcuts?"

I couldn't imagine how a boat forty-five feet long and ten feet wide could do a shortcut through the jungle.

Captain Joe must have noticed the baffled look on my face, so he pointed out one of the many streams flowing into the Purus.

"During the dry season, such a stream can accommodate nothing larger than a canoe. But during flood season, that stream can easily accommodate this and even bigger boats."

That conversation, and an afternoon cup of tea with Joe and Marjory, brought a welcome change from routine. It was now our third day on the water, and day five in Brazil. In spite of the slowness, we were a few hundred miles up the Purus River.

Gerson spread the word that sometime tomorrow we would arrive in Tapauá. This information sent the ten Americans into busy mode. Word also circulated that we were having pizza, instead of beans and rice, for dinner. This brought cheers from everyone. In the hours before dinner, everyone began describing his or her favorite pizza. The descriptions were elaborate, such as the deep-dish Italian sausage from My Pie, the thin crust supreme from Donelli's, and the four-cheese pizza from southern Brazil. The imagery stoked our appetites, as did the delicious smell wafting up from the galley. We were ravenous by the time three large baking trays were pulled from the oven and brought to the metal sundeck. As they were being cut, Calvin's flashlight illuminated the toppings.

"What!" we said in unison. Our lovely pizza was covered in anchovies, peas, and carrots.

"Who ever heard of canned vegetables and fish on pizza," Calvin grumbled.

"When in Rome . . ." Todd said, devouring his slice.

There was much less anticipation for the second batch of pizza to exit the oven. As we waited, Gerson called us over to speak in private with Bráulia. Whispering closely so others would not hear, Gerson relayed a concern Bráulia had presented to him. She was troubled by the fact that our team of five was one woman and four men.

"Why is this a problem?" Todd asked.

"Indians kill men, not women," was Bráulia's mind-reeling reply.

"Oh crap!" Calvin exclaimed as he rolled his head back in disbelief.

I was stunned by Bráulia's statement.

Todd glared at Gerson to confirm whether this was true. Then he turned to Bráulia and questioned in disbelief, "But you lived in the tribe already?"

"Yes, but we were only girls."

"What she means is," Gerson intervened, "that we just need to take one other girl so the tribe doesn't mistake us for warriors coming to attack them." Gerson explained that on previous trips men had hiked in most of the way but then let the girls enter the village.

I tried to be dispassionate and cross-examine like a journalist, "Was the tribe violent when you lived with them?"

"No. But I don't know what might happen should they see us on the trail," she said.

"You said a government anthropologist visited them," Calvin charged accusingly, pointing his finger like a prosecuting attorney.

"One man don't kill, but four man . . ."

She left us hanging on that unfinished sentence.

Gerson tried to defuse the situation by taking charge. "This is what we will do. Before breakfast tomorrow each of us needs to ask God if we should hike in to the tribe."

My body and emotions quavered under the surface, *What have I gotten into?*

Gerson summed up, "If two or more men choose to hike in, then we will ask another girl on the boat to join us. It is really a minor change in plans."

While we were calming down over our second slice of pizza, Todd must have sensed that Bráulia felt attacked by our "shoot the messenger" response.

"Bráulia, you're amazing," he said. "Tell us how you first went to this tribe."

She fixed a gaze on each of us, as if to verify it was safe. She began in a subdued manner, "They are called the Suruwahá."

She told us how hearing the news of a primitive tribe had gripped her heart. "Could I, as a single nineteen-year-old Brazilian girl, be the first missionary to make contact with this tribe?"

Bráulia prayed for most of that year and then requested others at YWAM Belém to pray with her. One single guy and a single girl joined her. She recounted how they had to hitch rides on boats up remote rivers. After many days of travel and waiting, a riverboat trader dropped them off at the stream leading to the Suruwahá. The trader was going even farther upriver to trade with the semi-primitive Dení Indians for rubber, tree oils, Brazil nuts, salted meat, and fish.

The team of three then hiked through thick jungle. After some days they found a well-worn trail, so they knew they were close. At this point the man on their team turned back to base camp while the two girls continued, arriving later that day.

Bráulia described the moment the Indians welcomed her.

"On that first night in the giant village house we were so happy that we just lay in our hammocks singing praise songs." Bráulia talked for hours, describing how the Suruwahá lived, hunting for food using blowguns with poison-tipped darts, or bows and arrows for large game.

Once in bed, I stared at galaxies of stars that remained motionless as we churned upriver. Now awakened to the facts, I couldn't stop thinking. What if Suruwahá men, while hunting hours from the village, encountered us on the trail? Would they panic and shoot us full of arrows?

I wasn't sure if I was on the most exciting adventure of my life or an ill-fated voyage to my death. I tried to hear from God whether I should hike in to the tribe, but I couldn't—my mind and emotions were garbled and confused. The one thing I did recall with utter clarity was a book I had read about Jim Elliot,[1] who led a team of five men to the Auca Indians back in the 1950s. Their first contact was peaceful.

However, now we know that the Auca Indians believed all outsiders to be cannibals. And since it was five men, it was assumed they were a war party. So the next time the missionaries met the Auca, they were ambushed and killed. I was wishing right then that I hadn't read the Jim Elliot story. In cases like these, ignorance really is bliss.

I forced my mind to think sensibly. Maybe some of us should stay back. "Better safe than sorry," my parents used to say. Yet spending so much time and money only to stay on the boat seemed ridiculous. But of course, getting killed because of cross-cultural assumptions would be even more ridiculous. I didn't mind taking a risk, even risking my life for an important cause, but I hated the thought of dying by mistake.

Every dramatic scene played over and over in my mind as the engine droned on and the night got blacker. Soon the morning light burned my bleary eyes. It seemed early, but it was already after 7:00 a.m. It looked as if everybody was up but me.

After moving my belongings into the tiny cabin, I waited for the one toilet on the boat. I was left with twenty-five minutes to make a life-or-death decision. Feeling tired and rushed was not helping. Considering the drama of the situation, I contemplated doing the dramatic thing—like randomly opening my Bible and reading where it opened. Then, on second thought, I decided to do my normal daily routine of reading one psalm, one proverb, and one chapter each from the Old Testament and New Testament.

Today's reading was Psalm 56. "When I am afraid, I will trust in you. In God, whose word I praise, in God I trust; I will not be afraid. What can mortal man do to me?"

"Thank you, God," I said out loud. The engine roar was so loud nobody could hear me, so I said out loud again, "Yeah, what can mortal man do to me?" It was the perfect verse for my situation. God spoke! His word brought instant peace to my heart.

We met at breakfast. Having such clear direction, I shared first. I didn't go into details, I simply said that I prayed and God confirmed it was right for me to hike in to the Suruwahá. Todd said yes. Calvin said yes. Gerson said yes.

"Is anyone sick or have a cold?" Bráulia asked sternly.

"No," everyone said.

"The flu can wipe out a tribe because they have no immunities," she lectured.

We assured her that we were all fine.

"OK then . . . we need another girl on the team," was Bráulia's decisive verdict.

I observed Gerson and Bráulia canvassing the two Brazilian girls on Alcír's team, but neither wanted to go to the Suruwahá. However, five of the seven girls on the American team wanted to go. These facts worried me. Three were dismissed because they were not physically able to hike sixty miles. The first interviewed was a fit thirty-five-year-old mother. The next was a nineteen-year-old named Tisha, who had straight blond hair and the physique of a track and field athlete. After a short debate it was decided that the younger of the two had a better chance of completing the arduous hike.

The decision was made and our team was set.

SIX

Up a Creek

SIX days had passed. One day in Belém, one day flying to Manaus and shopping, one day moving onto the boat, loading supplies, and getting under way. Then it was three more days up the Amazon and Purus Rivers to the town of Tapauá. I was impressed. Right on time, according to Gerson's itinerary.

Unlike the ramshackle villages we passed along the Purus River, Tapauá was a proper town. The YWAM house was next to the port we pulled into. The house clearly had not been painted for years, maybe decades. Local porters swarmed the American team to carry their bags. It was nice to get off the boat and just walk. Tapauá had concrete roads, a few dozen vehicles, and an airstrip. Gerson said there was a phone too, if we wanted to call home.

"Really? It's August 20—Josephine's birthday—do you think I could call her?" I was feeling terrible about missing her birthday after only six months of marriage.

"Sure, why not," Gerson said.

I was pumped. Josephine loved hearing she was loved; so a surprise call from the middle of the jungle would be a memorable birthday gift. We walked ten minutes to a small brick building that had TeleAmazon painted in man-sized letters across a wall. There was a long line of people waiting their turn for the phone. The person on the phone was sitting at a counter speaking into an old microphone.

"Look. The phone is actually a radio," Calvin said with a snicker, "and everyone can hear what's being said. How funny is that!"

Todd chuckled too, but I didn't, as I realized it could be an hour or two before I got a turn. Gerson made the same deduction and turned to leave. Dejected, I followed him out. We walked to a house with a café area where I overindulged in guaraná and deep-fried banana chips while Gerson described Tapauá as a typical rural town.

"Most rural people in the Amazon identify themselves as Ribeirinhos," he said. "There are ten times more Ribeirinhos in the Amazon than tribal people."

"Are the Ribeirinho people Brazilians?" Calvin questioned.

"Yes, but they're different." Gerson explained how thousands of Portuguese entered the Amazon in the mid-1800s intent on getting rich collecting rubber. Those who stayed on after 1912, the year the price of rubber collapsed ending the Amazon's Golden Age, became known as Ribeirinhos because they settled in the floodplain of the edges of the Amazon and its many tributaries.

"*Ribeirinho* can be translated as 'River People,'" Gerson continued. "They are like those French-speaking people who live in the swamps of the Mississippi River near New Orleans."

"The Cajuns?" Todd suggested.

"Yes, the Cajuns. The River People are a lot like the Cajuns—subsistence fishermen, hunters, and farmers in a world dominated by water and forest."

"Are the River People then a Brazilian subculture, like the Cajuns are an American subculture?" Todd asked.

"Exactly," Gerson affirmed. "They are not indigenous, but neither are they modern Brazilians. Hundreds of church denominations focus on Brazilians in the cities and towns while dozens of mission agencies focus on tribes. But only one mission agency that I know of, called

Project Amazon, focuses on the River People. God willing, with YWAM, that will be two."

We shoved off midafternoon. I was surprised to see Alcír remain on the boat. Because he was the team leader in Tapauá, I assumed he would stay there. But since Baia and Edilberto spoke better English than Alcír, they took charge of the American team. Gerson said he and Alcír would do the night driving while Captain Joe and Marjory would continue with their day shift.

I awoke at dawn on day seven to the familiar sight of a wall of trees. I was told we had exited the Purus in the night and turned due west onto the Tapauá River, yet another liquid artery that brought us ever deeper into the heart of the jungle.

Late morning on day eight, Alcír walked by, combing his thick black hair and wiping his eyes in between yawns. He could have slept only a few hours. Soon Bráulia passed by with Brazilian espressos. We didn't normally have a midmorning coffee. Todd asked Captain Joe, "What's up?"

"No highway signs to show the way," Joe said with a laugh. Then more seriously he said, "You don't want to get lost in the Amazon."

As we sipped the strong, sweet espresso, Captain Joe explained that only Alcír and Bráulia had been to this place before.

"The large lake we are crossing right now is actually the merged Cunhuá and Tapauá Rivers," Joe said. "Instead of two distinct rivers up ahead, there are seven different channels. Three of the splinter channels go for many miles before they dead-end with no outlet. Ending up down one of these channels would be the worst-case scenario."

We each held down a corner of a map as Captain Joe pointed out where we were. "We are fortunate to be here in daylight," Joe said, "because if it was night we would get lost for sure."

Alcír shut off the engine a couple times to assess the direction and strength of the current, and after a couple hours the Cunhuá River channel was distinguished from the other six. Once again Captain Joe was confident of our way ahead. As night fell, the boat's high-beam spotlights scanned right and left like a police helicopter, keeping us in the center of the river channel. We roared on through the night.

The slowness of seven days of river travel seemed like weeks. We were now on a tributary of a tributary of a tributary of the Amazon River. It was the third month of the five-month dry season, and the farther we went up, the narrower and shallower the rivers became. If we found the right drop-off spot, we would hike into the Suruwahá village tomorrow. Although everyone was confident they had heard the word of the Lord, the possibility of being mistaken for a war party and getting shot full of arrows was still a recurring thought. Calvin wasn't taking any chances, so he decided to pray and fast.

After breakfast I joined Calvin in prayer on the metal sun deck. By late morning, after we finished praying, Calvin pointed into the water and said, "Hey, I can see the bottom." As if on cue, the boat lurched as if it had braked. I could feel, then see, the boat rise on top of a sand bar as the engine still roared, straining to carry us forward. No longer fully supported by water, the boat lost buoyancy and began a danger- ous slow-motion lean to the left. Instinctively everyone ran right and attempted to extend our weight over the edge like we were sailing an ocean catamaran. The propeller was then engulfed by sand. With a bang, like steel hitting steel, the engine stopped. The sudden silence stunned us. No one moved, yet momentum shoved the boat forward like an invisible hand. I was holding my breath as the bow pointed slightly downward. The boat creaked and groaned like a mortally wounded beast ready to fall to its side and die. But then, as if it had changed its mind, it slid forward and we were floating once again.

After assessing our surroundings and consulting the maps, Cap- tain Joe determined that we had entered a fork of the river that went nowhere. That meant we had to somehow get back over the sandbar to the Cunhuá River. I had no idea how that was going to happen.

Soon Captain Joe, Gerson, and Alcír were in the water. They walked the length of the sand bar looking for a section deep enough for the boat to get across but it was consistently shallow. The deepest spot of the sand bar was the V-shaped channel that the boat had created as it pushed over. We were sort of up a creek without a paddle. After a coffee and some deliberations, Captain Joe announced that the only way to get out was to back the boat into the same spot we came over and carve a large channel by using the boat's propeller churning in reverse. He started the engine then shouted, "Full speed backward!"

Sure enough, great swirls of sand were thrust forward as the propeller began tunneling us backward. It churned and churned for almost three hours. Sometime after lunch we were freed back into the Cunhuá River once again.

The engine now ran at half speed because of the shallowness of the water. Captain Joe's eyes shifted continuously between the depth finder and the river in front for fear of straying out of the deep and hitting bottom.

"The water level is dropping quickly now. We'll make it to the trailhead," Joe said, "but after your three-day hike, I am not sure if we will get out of here again."

Captain Joe had the unusual skill of delivering bad news in a cheerful sort of way. "Manaus is a thousand miles inland and we are nearly another thousand miles farther up four rivers from Manaus. If the river gets too shallow, we'll be stuck up here until Christmas!"

The next day Gerson told us to get our packs ready because we might get to the trailhead sometime in the night. "That would be perfect," he said. "It would allow us to leave at dawn and to make the long hike in one day."

As evening fell, I heard the bellow of howler monkeys calling their troop together for the night. I initiated my own bedtime routine early. I wanted to be rested and ready for the hike ahead. I realized I had never hiked sixty miles over three days. Yet, at twenty-five years old I was in my physical prime, so in that respect I was confident.

As I lay trying to go off to sleep, I marveled at the fact that I was here—the Amazon jungle! I wasn't just flying over it. I was in it—the heart of it—some two thousand miles from where I had landed ten days earlier. Like the books said, it was dense, tropical, exotic, and insect-infested, interlaced by waterways teeming with friendly fish, killer fish, electric eels, alligators, snakes, and dangers unimaginable. In a few hours I would be hiking through these dangers. More than that, I would be making contact with a primitive tribe, something few humans in history have done.

I prayed for God to help and protect me. As I closed my eyes, I recited the verse God gave me for this situation, "In God I trust; I will not be afraid. What can mortal man do to me?"

PART TWO

Tribal and River People

I will praise you, O Lord, among the nations;
I will sing of you among the peoples.

PSALM 108:3

Into the Jungle

I WOKE before dawn. The sunrise was barely a visible glow behind us as we traveled west into the darkness. Alcír was alone at the wheel, allowing Gerson a full night of sleep before the arduous hike. With the engine at half roar I could hear the bow cutting through the narrow river. Slowly others awoke. Breakfast was the usual—strong coffee and crackers with a thin spread of margarine. Everyone ate except Calvin, who refused due to his commitment to fasting. I joined Calvin once again in prayer. Because of the time zone difference, I calculated that our Australian church, Parkside Baptist, had probably prayed for me six hours ago. In six more hours my home church, Redeemer Lutheran, would be praying for me, and then two hours after that, Josephine and our church in LA would also pray.

Some hours passed, and the scorching equatorial sun was high in the sky. A pair of blue-and-yellow macaws squawked loudly as they flew overhead. Just then the engine dropped to a low rumble.

"We're here," Bráulia announced.

The stream mouth looked about as wide as our boat and maybe two feet deep. A quick survey confirmed there was no chance of getting closer to the Suruwahá village, so Captain Joe gently guided the *São Mateus* onto the sand. Gerson clambered out the window of the big room and onto the bank. I suggested a quick lunch before leaving, but Gerson was already yelling, "Let's get going! If we hurry we still might make it today." I grabbed the homemade granola trail mix my thoughtful wife had made and threw it into my daypack. Within a minute we were on the sand smiling for a picture.

Captain Joe said something to Gerson about doing maintenance on the boat for an hour or two before leaving to visit a family that Alcír had met during his last trip to the area. "We will rendezvous back here in three days," he added.

"God bless you," Joe and Marjory then said in unison. With that, we turned and walked into Suruwahá country.

We set out at a fast pace: Gerson at the front, Bráulia next with Tisha beside her, then Todd and Calvin, and finally me at the rear. The jungle is home to wild pigs, snakes, pumas, jaguars, and more. Gerson had explained in one of our team meetings that the man in the front carried the shotgun while the man at the back carried the machete, because jaguars attack from the rear. Now that I was at the back wielding a rather insignificant blade, I was thinking, *Shouldn't I be the one with the shotgun?*

Everyone carried a daypack with an instant soup packet for food, two bottles of water, a sheet for sleeping, and a few dry clothes, knowing we would get hot and sweaty in the brutal jungle humidity. Tied on the outside of our daypacks were our hammocks and ropes. The simple Brazilian hammock I bought in Manaus weighed about five pounds, but the jungle hammocks Calvin and Todd had bought at a second-hand military store in LA had mosquito-netting sidewalls and a roof and were fully rubberized. They must have weighed twenty pounds. Todd lashed his on top of his daypack while Calvin tied his underneath. With every step, the twenty-pound hammock swung out, then banged against Calvin's lower back. After twenty minutes he couldn't bear it anymore, so he stopped to retie. Ten minutes later he stopped to retie again. Ten minutes after that, he untied it completely and threw it down on the trail. "It's too heavy to carry," he said. "I'll sleep on the ground."

After hiking briskly for about an hour, we came to a large clearing made by Brazilian government workers when they marked the borders of the Suruwahá land. It was a clearing because it had no trees, but clear it was not. It was now overgrown with all sorts of underbrush. The trail emptied right into this tangled mess, with no exit in sight. An abandoned hut that had lost its thatch roof stood in the midst of the thicket, so we headed in that direction. But everyone got so terribly tangled up and snarled in bristles that we literally got stuck!

"I'm going to try to skirt around this," I yelled to the others.

"Go for it," Calvin said. "The trail has to be here somewhere."

As I untangled myself, I pulled my right arm through a cluster of tall grass that stuck to my skin like an octopus tentacle. As I pulled away from the innocuous looking green grass, it literally tore my skin off. It left me bleeding like I had been scratched by a cat. Then each of the four bloody stripes began burning like someone had poured salt in my wound. As I ranted in pain, Bráulia realized my plight and warned everyone, "Be careful of fire vine."

Then Todd yelled out in pain as a thorn caught his ear. It refused to let go as he walked by, tearing open the top of his ear. I continued backing out. I got tangled a second time and emerged with my pants torn in two places. Gerson also backed out, but the other four were now marooned on the frame of the abandoned hut. Gerson told them to wait there. He and I made forays into the jungle, looking for the trail's continuation, but to no avail. Finally Gerson approached me, "Captain Joe said he might be at the bank for a couple of hours. I'm thinking if you ran back to the river you might catch the boat before they leave. You could bring Alcír back, who probably remembers the way. Do you think you could do that?"

The trail was clear and easy coming in, so I said, "No worries, I can do that."

"OK, great. Try to be quick."

I hadn't paid much attention to the trail hiking in because I was at the back following everyone in front. I knew the river was north, but the sun was so straight up in the sky that I couldn't tell which direction was east or west by looking at it. Soon I was feeling unsure, but I kept running anyway. After about thirty minutes I was happy to arrive at the river but disappointed to see it was vacant. The boat had left.

I was now excessively hot and sweaty. I stripped to my boxers and dove into the cool water. I took a long cool drink straight from the river; it was so refreshing, but there was no time to lose. The team was waiting. Then I realized my arm was bleeding into the river and I could be attacked by piranha, crocodiles, an anaconda, or God knows what else. I was out of that river in an instant.

My stupidity of going into the river bleeding started a chain of dreadful thoughts. My first thought was of an anaconda leaping out of the water at me, so I moved away from the river's edge to dress. Moments later, jogging back the way I came, I thought of getting attacked by a jaguar, so I kept looking behind me as I ran. I was kicking myself for not bringing the machete, not that it would help much against a jaguar. Then I began to fear getting lost. Every twist in the trail required a decision and soon nothing looked familiar. When you are alone, you really doubt yourself. I recalled Captain Joe solemnly saying, "You don't want to get lost in the Amazon."

After forty minutes of anxiety, but without mishap, I made it back.

"Sorry, guys, the boat was already gone."

"That's OK, Kent. I'm sure we'll be fine," Todd said.

I sat down in the shade and closed my eyes, allowing the anxiety of almost getting lost to melt away. After regaining my composure, I asked, "So, where's Gerson?"

"He's still looking for the trail. We just need to wait," Bráulia said.

It was after one o'clock and we had made less than one hour of progress. But inside I really didn't care because I was happy just to be back with the team and not lost in the jungle.

Sometime after two o'clock Gerson returned announcing he had found the trail, so we set off once again at a brisk pace. I'd had a cool dip in the river, but the four who had sat in the blazing tropical sun for almost two hours were sunburned, weak, and feeling heat exhaustion.

The trail brought us back into the shade, but it was still incredibly hot. Numerous trees were across the trail. Some were so monstrous they made Minnesota's Norway pines look like shrubs. On some occasions we literally had to boost one another to the top of the tree trunk and then slide down the other side.

After four hours of hiking, it was beginning to get dark. The sun rises and sets at six on the equator, and we were only six degrees south. When we arrived at a natural open space near a stream, Gerson announced we would stay here for the night. "Get your hammocks up," he said. "It will be dark soon."

We set up camp by tying our hammocks to suitable trees around the edge of the clearing. Todd and I went foraging for dry wood. By the time we returned, Tisha and Bráulia had created a fire pit. Gerson struck a match against the box sandpaper strip only to see the match head crumble into mush. They had absorbed Gerson's perspiration right through his pack and were useless.

"I guess we should have borrowed the butane lighter off the boat," Todd said dryly.

"Hmm, too late for that now," Gerson mumbled.

Our clothes were soaked with perspiration, so everyone eagerly changed into dry sleeping clothes, everyone, that is, except for Calvin. He had a pounding headache and no hammock, so he just flopped onto the ground, longing for the mercy of sleep. But he was shown no mercy by the ants. They found him on the ground and swarmed his hot and sweaty body like a giant picnic morsel. He leapt up and writhed out of his T-shirt. We watched helplessly as Calvin slapped away ferocious little biting ants.

"Looks like the slap dance he learned in Samoa as a missionary," Todd quipped.

We tried not to, but we couldn't help but laugh, as Calvin frantically dashed for the nearby stream slapping his body. Upon Calvin's return the two girls offered one of their hammocks for him to sleep in, explaining that they would sleep together in one. His chivalrous attempt at refusing lasted about five seconds and then he took up their offer.

Dinner was a tasteless, undissolved instant soup floating in unheated water.

While on the boat, Gerson had told us that jungle animals wouldn't bother us in the night for fear of the fire. Since we had no fire, the assumption was obvious. As darkness descended, the jungle became loud with chirps, creaks, hoots, and howls. Gerson assured us the shotgun was loaded and that he would protect us against any night intruders. I lay awake for a while, trying to figure out how Gerson would ward off an attacking animal in the pitch-blackness with our five hammocks spread around a large area. I calculated there was a better chance of getting accidently shot and killed by Gerson than attacked by a jungle animal. But I was so tired that even fear and adrenaline couldn't keep me awake. I slept soundly all night.

Hazards of the Trail

W E left camp about 7:00 a.m. Bráulia said we were about halfway, which I found encouraging. She warned, however, that the second part of the trail was hilly. I soon discovered that *hilly* wasn't the right word. Maybe it was her limited English; in any case, I felt like we were climbing mountain slopes. It was a steep crawl up and just as steep down, then across a stream at the bottom. The oppressive heat and humidity made the hike far more difficult than we had expected.

There were many streams. Most had carved deep gullies, leaving sheer five- to ten-foot embankments, which were very difficult to get up. Wherever we could, we crossed over the gullies on fallen logs that spanned the gap. One such log was so slippery with green moss that Todd decided to crawl rather than walk. Halfway across, the rotting log broke under his weight and catapulted him into the stream below. It was a miracle that the log didn't crush him or that he didn't break a bone in the fall.

About twenty miles into the hike it became apparent that Calvin was near the point of utter exhaustion. He drank and rested at every stream, then rested halfway up the hill and again at the peak. The gap between the three in front and the three of us at the back had widened considerably. At yet another stream Todd and I scrambled up the gully embankment, but Calvin could not make it. He walked upstream some distance to a less steep portion and tried again, but the soil collapsed from under him, sending him tumbling backward into the dirt with a heavy thump.

"I can't make it!" he raged in disappointment.

Todd and I scuttled back down the embankment to his side. Then he repeated, "I can't make it." But this time it was an admission of defeat. Calvin remained on his back. Todd and I looked at each other, each hoping the other would know what to do. Turning around meant twenty miles back to the river, which Calvin clearly could not do, but neither could he keep going. Calvin was down for the count. After a few moments I volunteered to run ahead to the other three, who were not aware of the predicament. Todd said, "Go."

It took me at least thirty minutes to catch them, as the slopes were too steep to run up. When I finally caught up, I explained the situation. It was decided that Todd and I should help Calvin get to a clearing I had just passed through. We would rest in that clearing, then decide what to do. I half ran, half walked back and found Calvin lying in the stream, allowing cool water to glide over him. After I relayed the plan, Calvin was adamant that he could not continue; he just wanted to stay there, lying in the cool water.

"Come on, Calvin, the clearing is just ahead," I explained.

Todd had found an easier way up the gully bank and encouraged Calvin that he could make it, but he just lay there. After an anxious wait of some minutes, he finally stood up.

"My head is pounding," he said. "But at least I'm no longer dizzy. I shouldn't have fasted."

After a booster of granola, the three of us resumed the hike slowly. By the time we arrived, Gerson, Bráulia, and Tisha had been waiting in the clearing for well over an hour. It was nearly one in the afternoon. Calvin announced he could not continue. He apologized to everyone and volunteered to stay in the jungle by himself. Todd insisted on staying with him, but Calvin insisted otherwise. Todd relented, but only on the condition that Calvin take his hammock and the shotgun. Gerson agreed.

"We should be back in twenty-four hours," Gerson said.

"I should be good by then," Calvin said as he flopped into the hammock.

"We need to make it to the tribe tonight," Gerson said. With that we resumed our hike at a brisk pace.

"Don't forget how to get back here!" was Calvin's panicked afterthought as we disappeared down the trail.

By five in the evening we knew we were close. The trail had become wide and noticeably worn. Bráulia stopped and reminded us that the Suruwahá would be super inquisitive and potentially take whatever we had, so she instructed us not to bring anything we were unwilling to lose or have broken. I had a recorder to record their language. I decided to hang on to it and everything else in my pack. Todd, on the other hand, decided to leave his glasses. He was afraid that if they were taken, he wouldn't be able to hike out of the jungle. He left them on the ground behind a tree stump, along with a camera he had borrowed from his father-in-law. We marked the spot with machete hacks into trees on each side of the trail.

Soon we approached a large clearing that Bráulia said was the Suruwahá plantation. We stopped at the edge. She would go first because the tribe would recognize her. We would follow once we heard the commotion of the encounter. As Bráulia left, Todd started praying while I turned on my recorder and made this introduction:

"Today is Monday, August 26, and it is approximately five p.m. We are about to enter the Suruwahá. We have spent sixteen hours on the trail these last two days. We hope, and pray, for a pleasant encounter with this primitive tribe. If not . . . well . . . I love you, Josephine."

Soon Bráulia shouted out greetings in the Suruwahá language. In response we heard yelling and commotion. I couldn't discern if the sounds were friendly or hostile because they were so different.

Tisha overheard my recording and looked at me with alarm. She had been nonchalant about everything thus far, but now fear hit her. I felt bad we hadn't prepared this teenager for what we were about to experience.

I wasn't sure I was prepared myself.

A Primal Encounter

A FEW steps into the plantation I saw a huge cone-like structure towering over banana trees. It was the *maloca*, the tribe's impressive communal home. Walking closer, I could now hear that the sounds beyond the banana trees were intermingled with laughter. A hundred feet ahead I saw the first Suruwahá. A man with golden-brown skin glistening in the sunlight stared at us. He was about five foot five with a strong, stocky build. His hair was charcoal black with a peculiar bowl-shaped cut. As we emerged from the plantation, groups of Suruwahá men, women, and children converged on each of us.

We were a very unusual spectacle to them. Gerson and Todd drew attention because of their height. Soon everyone was taking turns touching Gerson's dark skin and his Afro hair. Tisha's almost shimmering white-gold hair got even more attention. Their curiosity was almost overwhelming, examining everything we were wearing and carrying. They tried to get my daypack open but did not understand a zipper. I unzipped it for them, which drew gasps and giggles from all around.

Soon everything in my pack was on the ground. My sugarless gum was found and tried, no doubt for the first time in Suruwahá history. They seemed to like it. Next they tried my wife's yummy homemade granola, but reacted like it was the worst thing they had ever tasted, spitting out every last tiny grain and seed.

The Suruwahá gathered around each of us in mobs. I wasn't quite sure what their thoughts were, but they clearly thought we were funny. They laughed and pointed at us. I too could not help but laugh. Many of the youth seemed to gather around me, with their parents standing farther back observing. It could have been a scene from church camp or youth group except for the fact that everyone was naked. Well, ninety-nine percent naked. A G-string around their hips held up the men, while the women's G-string sported a small collection of tassels, which didn't even come close to forming a skirt.

I said "Kent" a number of times and pointed at myself until they understood it was my name. The Suruwahá had trouble pronouncing it, and it came out as Ketz. I had trouble saying their names too, as their language seemed an incomprehensible babble. When I tried to repeat the name of one young man, they laughed and pointed at me saying, "*Danyzy, danyzy.*" I asked Bráulia the meaning of that, and she said it meant "stupid."

One of the boys investigated my water bottle by upending it. When the last drops of water came out, he said "*Baau-mi*" to his friend. I repeated the word *baau-mi* and motioned with my hand like I was drinking water. A couple young kids were sent scampering off to the maloca and shortly returned with gourds of water. Since I'd learned the word for water, I told Tisha, Todd, and Gerson my discovery. Soon we were all drinking baau-mi out of gourds.

Then I made a motion toward my stomach like I was hungry. Once again body language worked. Soon a group of teenage boys came from the maloca with a large clay pot that took two to carry. I invited Todd and Gerson to come and eat, but they decided to head into the maloca.

I sat on a log ready to eat as they filled the water gourd with warm banana mush. Instead of giving it to me, one of the young adult boys lifted the gourd above me and started to pour it out. I opened my mouth to catch it, but he didn't stop until it overflowed my mouth and spilled down onto my chest. Everyone laughed. As I cleaned myself off, I saw Todd and Gerson running.

"Bráulia!" Gerson yelled as he veered toward her.

Todd ran to me. I stared at Todd as a Suruwahá warrior emerged from the maloca with bow and arrow in hand. I heard urgency in Gerson's voice as he yelled for Bráulia a second time. Todd tried to act calm as he reentered the crowd around me but his face told me he feared something dreadful was about to happen.

"He shot at us," Todd whispered.

I suddenly could feel each individual heart palpitation. I had read too many missionary martyr stories to cling to any sense of optimism at this moment.

The warrior had a six-foot-long arrow in his bow and came toward us like he was stalking an animal. He looked intensely at Bráulia and yelled something. We looked to Bráulia for translation, but she shook her head in incomprehension. When he returned his focus to Todd and me, a chill rippled through my body. Unaware of what was happening, Tisha's big green eyes darted, questioning if something was wrong.

The whole crowd became absolutely silent. Then, as if on cue, everyone burst out laughing. The warrior put down his weapon and launched into the Suruwahá version of sidesplitting laughter.

Noticeably relieved, Todd muttered, "I thought we were dead."

"What happened?" Tisha demanded as she came near, thinking she'd missed a great joke.

"A warrior returned from the hunt just as Gerson and I walked into the maloca," Todd recounted. "While our eyes were adjusting to the darkness inside, we saw him looking frantically around. He suddenly raised his bow and shot an arrow right between our heads. I made a beeline back here while Gerson went straight for Bráulia. The warrior strode out right behind us. I thought we were going to die."

Tisha's teenage face froze, her hand covering her gaping mouth, and her eyebrows at maximum elevation. I think she was unsure if she should scream in horror or laugh at our good fortune. Having experienced emotions so turbulent and confusing, I too felt stuck between those two extremes. But the laughter gave hope that we were safe with the Suruwahá.

The Maloca

W I T H the first encounter over, everyone moved into the tribe's communal home. The Brazilians call it the *maloca*, but the Suruwahá called it the *uda*. It was round and, by my estimation, about seventy-five feet across and seventy-five feet high. This is where all 119 Suruwahá lived. I was amazed they could construct something so large without hammer and nails. In fact, I would have thought a crane was necessary to elevate the four long poles that went to the top. The thatch roof was formed from thousands of neatly folded palm fronds, with one frond neatly laid an inch farther up from the frond under it, creating a tight and lightweight roof that could withstand strong wind and the heaviest tropical downpour.

I didn't know what to expect as I entered. It was dark and smoky inside. Everyone lived around the perimeter, with the center empty. It was laid out in nine big sections created by square frames of tree-trunk poles. Each pole was about six feet high and strung up with hammocks. It looked like each family had their own fire. They fed us the same banana mush I had outside. It tasted like warm banana custard, delicious and satisfying. One family shared bird meat with us, while another family shared some pork. They fed us until we could eat no more. I was dehydrated from the hike, and again the word for water was understood, so I drank deeply of baau-mi.

The Suruwahá hammocks were soft and, Bráulia told us, intricately woven from palm fiber. The husband's hammock was more than ten feet long, while the wife's hammock, strung just below her husband's, was slightly smaller. The children's small hammocks were lower still, unless there was a baby; its tiny hammock was right next to the mother's.

Todd and I were allocated a spot near a young family. I set up my hammock, but Todd's jungle hammock was with Calvin, so he had nothing to sleep in. Bráulia tried to explain that Todd needed a hammock but this seemed to create a dilemma. A group of Suruwahá men gathered in the middle to talk.

"What did they say?" Todd asked.

"They do not have any spare hammocks. They take months to make, so for that reason, they only have hammocks for as many people as there are," Bráulia said.

Finally, a family combined two of their children into one hammock for the night, providing an extra hammock for Todd. Although it was a child-size hammock, it was still strong enough to hold him. When Todd got into it, next to my big adult hammock, the Suruwahá pointed and laughed.

As we prepared to sleep, we pulled out our sheets to cover us. I had a plain white sheet but Todd's sheet was a bold pattern of red, white, blue, and yellow stripes. Soon a crowd gathered, feeling the fabric of Todd's sheet. Suddenly, one of the young guys abruptly walked off with it. As Todd went to get help from Bráulia, the man who had brought the child hammock to Todd took it down and walked away with that too. Now Todd was without a hammock or a sheet.

Five minutes later a group of men came from across the maloca and unfurled Todd's sheet, which now had twisted vine ropes at each corner. The sheet was tied to the poles, completing the transformation of Todd's sheet into a bigger and more comfortable hammock. With that, we settled down for an early night. But that was not to be, as Bráulia popped her head over our hammocks and said, "The Suruwahá want us to dance."

"You've got to be kidding," Todd remarked. "Now they'll shoot us for sure."

Bráulia directed us into the center of the maloca, where many Suruwahá formed a big circle around us. Not one of us, however, felt capable as dancers.

"Let's sing a few praise songs," Todd suggested.

"Yeah, we can do that!" came the reply.

We started worshiping loudly with a number of praise songs. When we came to the end, Gerson prayed out loud, still singing, as if it was another verse to the music. Bráulia followed suit, then all of us in turn. We sang prayers for the Suruwahá: we prayed for their spiritual blessing, we prayed for YWAM missionaries to work here, we prayed that the language could be learned sufficiently to preach the gospel. I sensed it was significant to pray these things out, right in their midst, right in their house. We were praising the Lord among the nations and singing of him among the peoples (Psalm 108:3).

After our singing, the Suruwahá seemed happy and congratulatory. It felt so good to lie down in the hammock again. I took long, deep breaths and could feel the gentle warmth of the small fire close by. After a series of long and satisfying yawns I closed my eyes and drifted toward sleep.

Moments later a cry for help jolted me awake.

"Bráulia, help!"

"What is it, Tisha?" Bráulia asked.

"Tell them to leave me alone!" Tisha pleaded.

I sat up in my hammock to see what was happening, but it was campfire dark inside, so I could not discern what was going on. Suddenly Tisha shrieked. I bolted out of my hammock and saw a young man with a knife next to Tisha. Fear struck again. The Suruwahá teenagers dispersed as the four of us converged on Tisha. She had her hammock held tightly to her face and whimpered, "They're trying to cut my hair!"

Tisha's long golden hair was obviously too tempting to resist for some of the boys and girls who wanted a souvenir. Already we could hear the Suruwahá parents scolding the offenders.

"It was probably a teenage dare," Todd said.

And so it seemed. With that we returned to our hammocks. I felt so drained and tired that I could hardly wait to close my eyes. I remembered a line from Psalm 62, the psalm I had read the morning we arrived at the trail, "Yes, my soul, find rest in God."

As I closed my eyes, I said a prayer of protection for my buddy Calvin, alone in the jungle. Then I thanked God for protecting our lives and fulfilling his word from Psalm 56, "What can mortal man do to me?"

ELEVEN

Alone in the Jungle

I T was comfortable sleeping in the impressive shelter. Pigs grunting outside and excessive bird chirping indicated it was dawn. The Suruwahá did not hurry to get up. After replenishing my dehydrated body with water the night before, I was bursting to use the toilet but I wasn't sure where to go. Finally some men started making their way out of the maloca. Todd and I had already decided to follow whoever left first. The male toilet, we soon discovered, was the edge of a large fallen tree. On one side, the men would stand and water the plants, on the other side were small smooth trees, allowing you something to hang onto while squatting. It was a very sanitary arrangement.

After the toilet stop we were brought down to the stream, where we washed and freshened up. Returning to the Suruwahá village, we saw a teenage boy hunting with a blowgun about seven feet long and with dozens of sharpened sticks in a mini quiver. These darts were as long as a fireplace match but as thin as toothpicks. I could see one dart ready in the blowgun as he scanned the sky for birds. A burst of air onto a cotton-like wad at the end of the dart could propel it beyond the tree tops—an amazing jungle technology.

We were with the Suruwahá a total of seventeen hours. We started to leave at about ten that morning, but the tribal women did not want Bráulia to go. They literally pulled her back down every time she got up to leave. We stood around for almost half an hour as Bráulia negotiated the leaving protocols with the women.

During this delay Tisha asked me for help to bandage her feet. When she took off her tennis shoes, I saw that her heels were bloody. Her canvas high-top tennis shoes were fashionable but not made for serious hiking, as the wet, heavy canvas had rubbed her heels raw. Tisha had torn a ring of fabric off the bottom of her T-shirt that I helped wrap like a bandage around the heel of each foot. It would be a painful thirty-mile hike for her.

Finally, Gerson and Todd literally pulled Bráulia from the grasp of the women. We started our hike about 10:30 a.m., and to my surprise about half the men in the village came with us. Five minutes down the track I saw that the teenage boy with the blowgun had killed a stunning red-and-blue Amazon macaw. He was pulling off feathers as we walked by. Back home these rare birds would be highly prized, yet to them it was lunch.

We arrived where Todd had left his glasses, camera, and watch. The Suruwahá walked very fast, and we were already falling behind, so Todd just grabbed his things and kept going. Soon he was doing the Samoan slap dance. Hundreds of ants that were on his camera were now all over his hands and arms.

After some moments he exclaimed, "The camera case!"

"Did you forget the camera case?" I asked.

"No, the ants ate it!"

Todd handed me his camera. It had two fine wires bouncing in front while still attached to the metal button pressed into the back. The wires and the button were all that was left of the wraparound vinyl case. Ants must have swarmed the case for the full seventeen hours, eating. Now Todd and I understood, with immense appreciation, how efficient the jungle ants are in breaking down whatever lands on the forest floor.

About an hour into our hike we came to an intersection of pathways, where most of the Suruwahá veered off. They had baskets and small spears, in addition to their bows and arrows, so Bráulia thought they were going to a stream to fish. However, about eight men continued to walk ahead of us.

We arrived back to Calvin almost exactly twenty-four hours after we left him. Calvin was looking good and feeling good. We thanked God for that. He was thrilled to meet the Suruwahá. Bráulia had been able to communicate that one man slept alone in the jungle, which apparently was the reason so many accompanied us. The Suruwahá wanted to meet this great warrior who was brave enough to sleep alone in the jungle, something they would never do. When Calvin heard that, he burst out laughing.

"Don't tell them this great warrior stayed up much of the night frightened like a baby."

Like ourselves the day before, we could see in Calvin the intense combination of fear and joyful excitement in meeting the Suruwahá. The Suruwahá men were amazed at Calvin's size and gathered pieces of vine from the jungle to measure his thighs and biceps. They tucked these under their G-string, no doubt to show the others back in the maloca how big the fearless warrior was.

Soon we were back on the trail. All eight Suruwahá had been in front, but after Calvin joined us, one Suruwahá man walked in front and another right behind Calvin. They clearly thought he was someone special. God was faithful to Calvin in bringing the Suruwahá to him when he couldn't get to them. This was not lost on Calvin. At one point he prophetically declared, "One day these people will walk this path worshiping God in their own language!"

Seeing Calvin animated and strong brought us all renewed strength. Todd and I recounted the hours we spent with the Suruwahá. Calvin was keeping up, and we worshiped the Lord with thanksgiving as we pressed on down the trail. Thankfully, today was significantly cooler than the two days hiking in. We hiked the hills at a steady clip and labored heavily under the exertion, yet not one of the Suruwahá even broke a sweat. At midafternoon, four of the eight Suruwahá turned back to the village while four remained with us, keeping us moving all day and getting us back to our first campground by 6:15 p.m.

Alcír had obviously hiked in to this campground, because a campfire was waiting for us. The boat crew must have been worried and come looking, since we'd missed our rendezvous deadline. Gerson calculated it was three more hours to the boat and suggested we keep going.

"I don't like the idea of hiking in the dark," Todd said.

"We can make it with the help of the Suruwahá and our flashlights," Bráulia assured us.

"I can't keep hiking another three hours," Calvin said.

Gerson, Bráulia, and Tisha were clearly intent on continuing, while Todd and Calvin had decided to stay the night in the jungle. I preferred to get back to the comfort and safety of the boat, but I didn't want to leave Calvin and Todd. Everyone looked at me. I decided to stay.

Since we had the light of a fire, we gave them our flashlights. They also took the shotgun. The four Suruwahá had no hammocks, so they left for the boat too, leaving us three inexperienced gringos alone in the jungle for the night.

Soon Todd was cocooned in his hammock while Calvin and I sat at the fire joking about roasting hot dogs, live dogs, or anything else that might wander into the camp. Calvin had fasted on the boat the day before we arrived at the trail, then he missed the ample feed given to us in the maloca. So having completed his fourth day with no food, he was ravenous. I too was hungry, and the conversation made me even hungrier.

In spite of previous complaints on the boat, we were now longing for the Brazilian beans and rice that the rest of the team would soon be having. This led to verbally kicking Gerson and Bráulia for telling us not to carry any food because of the weight. Todd stopped our complaining with a comment about the people of Israel longing for the leeks and onions of Egypt and for grumbling against Moses. "I think you better get in your hammock before the earth opens up and swallows you," he quipped.

We took Todd's advice by repenting and heading for bed. The problem was that Calvin and I had to share a hammock. Now we were kicking ourselves for not asking Tisha to leave her hammock so that we would each have one. We attempted again and again to find an equilibrium, but physics always won. Calvin was heavier than I was. This weight difference created a downward slope causing me to slowly slide into him. No matter how many times we readjusted, I always ended up sliding down.

Discomfort, however, turned into pure misery around nine o'clock in the form of rain. Our thin sheets offered little resistance against the tropical downpour. Calvin and I were soon soaked. Todd, on the other hand, was rewarded for his effort in carrying the twenty-pound jungle hammock. He remained dry and rested comfortably. Fifteen minutes passed. The rain was cold and unrelenting. Thirty minutes passed, and I was shivering uncontrollably. The rain had reduced our fire to a faint glow of embers.

"Calvin, I'm getting up to rescue the fire, otherwise I will freeze," I said.

Freezing, of course, was an exaggeration. But growing up in one of the coldest states in America, I could never remember shivering like this. I got up and stretched my body over the fire, protecting the remnant embers and letting the warmth melt away the cold. Calvin soon joined me, "This downpour is incredible. So much for not raining during dry season."

We took turns hanging our bodies over the fire like a protective roof and breathing life into the coals. We decided to untie our hammock and support it on poles over the fire. The heavy, wet hammock kept in the smoke and heat while serving as a roof for us. Our plan worked, but hour after hour, the rain continued. The poles fell to the side as we dozed off to sleep with the hammock falling right on top of the flame, but it was too saturated with rain to catch alight. We could not stay awake; however, when we dozed off, either the icy cold water on our back or the heat of the flame on our front would shock us awake again.

After five hours the ground no longer absorbed the deluge, leaving us sitting in a pool of cold, muddy water. We had to do something, so we decided to tie our hammock directly under Todd, who was about three feet off the ground, allowing his roof-covered hammock to protect us from the pelting rain. We tied the hammock as taut as we could, but as we feared, when the two of us got in, it slouched right to the ground. Our feet and knees were back in the cold muddy water. However, at this point, we were just too tired to care. The shelter of Todd's hammock protected from the rain, allowing us to sleep, off and on, for a few hours.

By seven o'clock it was light enough to see. The trail was slippery and slow, but the rain had subsided to a drizzle. We made it to the boat just after eleven that morning.

"Welcome back," Captain Joe said. "We've been praying for you."

"Thank you, we needed it. That was the longest night of my life," I replied.

Everybody on board was clean and rested, riding out the storm in the comfort and safety of the boat. The three of us looked like death warmed over by comparison. But we didn't care; we were safe and back with friends. We savored the strong Brazilian coffee and a banana like it was the first time we had ever eaten.

When the engine of the *São Mateus* roared to life once again, all I could think was *What a trip!* It was grueling and had pushed us to the point of utter physical and emotional exhaustion, yet it was worth it. It was a quest that few in history have made and one I would most likely never do again, unless, of course, God said otherwise.

TWELVE

Downstream through Time

THE all-night downpour raised the river level so substantially that getting stuck until Christmas was no longer a concern. However, the boat trip to the trailhead had taken an extra day, and the Suruwahá hike also took longer than planned. This meant there was no chance of making it back to Manaus in time to catch our flight to the United States. But it also meant that we now had a bit of extra time on the river. So the next morning we stopped to dig a few turtle eggs out of a sandy beach, which made for an amazing breakfast omelet. In the hot afternoon we stopped for a swim, despite Gerson's exaggerated warnings of man-eating piranha.

On the second day downstream, Captain Joe did a sideways maneuver and deftly docked alongside a raft of logs. A simple wooden plank house was built on top. Only the top quarter of the huge logs was above water, but that still placed the inhabitants at least two feet above getting wet. The raft was tethered to large trees to keep it from floating downriver. Inside were a grandpa, grandma, and a young mother who alternated between breastfeeding a newborn and a two-year-old. The two-year-old clung to his mother in fear.

In spite of being a trading post and general store, the only edible treat available was cans of caramel. So after everyone purchased one of those from the grandma, we shook the grandpa's hand as we stepped out the door. His long yellow nails and thick rough calluses made it feel like I was shaking the paw of a bear. Some hours later, back on the boat, I lay in my hammock for a siesta in the open room. I tried to sleep but could only think about the options before me.

In Manaus Gerson had expressed the need for a permanent YWAM base on the river. Then in Tapauá he described the River People and how there is only one mission agency for more than one million of them. Then we visited the Suruwahá to see if tribal ministry was the right fit for Josephine and me. These were our three ministry options: a YWAM base in Manaus, the River People, or tribal ministry. All options were incredibly challenging. Gliding swiftly downstream, I rocked gently in my hammock and drifted back through time.

Two months earlier, when Todd and Calvin had purchased their tickets to Brazil, they made a reservation for me on the same flight. I told them, as I had done earlier, that I didn't have the money for such a trip.

"Pray anyway and hear what God says," they insisted.

In response to their request, the next morning Josephine and I did just that. She went into the bedroom to seek God while I stayed in our living room and prayed. Some hours passed before Josephine said she was coming out. I volunteered to start.

"I did not receive a strong conviction of yes or no, but I got two verses."

"What are they?"

"The first is Isaiah 21, but I have to explain something first. One night, I stayed up late watching a documentary about gold mining in the Amazon. It was really horrible."

"You never told me about that."

"It was so harsh that it left me depressed and not wanting to go to the Amazon, so I didn't want to tell you. But then this morning, totally out of the blue, I read Isaiah 21. It so specifically described my feelings that I knew it was for me," I said.

"What does it say?" she asked.

"A harsh vision has been shown to me; the treacherous one still deals treacherously, and the destroyer still destroys . . . I am so bewildered I cannot hear, so terrified I cannot see. My mind reels, horror overwhelms me."[2]

"What does that mean?"

"I don't know. It's just how I felt after watching the TV program. But ever since, I have battled a fear about dying in the Amazon and everybody forgetting about me."

My face got hot. It sounded stupid hearing myself say that, and now Josephine didn't know what to say. A long, awkward silence followed.

"OK, that was one verse—you said you got two verses."

I flipped through the pages of the Bible until I found the second verse, then read it out: "She did what she could. She poured perfume on my body beforehand to prepare for my burial. I tell you the truth, wherever the gospel is preached throughout the world, what she has done will also be told, in memory of her."

Josephine looked down at her Bible then shrieked, "Me too! I got Mark 14 as well!"

"No way! Seriously?"

"Yes, Mark 14, verses 3 through 9," she confirmed. "God spoke to me especially through verse 3: A woman came with an alabaster jar of very expensive perfume, made of pure nard. She broke the jar and poured the perfume on his head."

After reading that, she looked me straight in the eye and said, "God spoke to me about the $600 of wedding money I was saving for special crockery. I think we should combine that with our regular monthly missionary support to buy the $900 airfare to Brazil."

"But I will still need to buy my round-trip ticket to Miami, which is another $300," I said.

Josephine nodded.

"Then I will need $300 for expenses in Brazil."

Josephine nodded again.

"Then if we use our mission support for the airfare instead of rent, we will need another $300 to pay our rent by the end of the month."

Josephine nodded a third time.

"That's another $900! If the second $900 doesn't appear out of thin air, we will lose the first $900."

We both sat in silence as we considered the implications. The faith step was radical, yet it seemed right. The guidance process, too, was out of the ordinary—seeking God's will for the future only to be convicted by the Holy Spirit regarding fears and finances, which somehow added up to guidance? I couldn't work it out in my brain, but strange guidance seemed to be a common experience for YWAM missionaries.

"You're right, sweetheart. I should go" I said. "God has spoken clearly."

With that, we bought the airfare from Miami to the Amazon. However, for the rest of the month no money came in.

It was July 31 and our rent was due. Josephine, who is an early riser, must have heard me stirring, because she soon bounded into the bedroom with a smile, a kiss, and a cup of tea.

"I am going to miss you," she said, staring intently into my eyes. She could always outstare me in our love stare, especially when I had sleep in my eyes.

"If a lot of money doesn't miraculously appear today, I won't be getting on the plane, and therefore you, Mrs. Kent Truehl, won't be missing me," I replied between sips of hot tea.

As newlyweds we were still getting used to each other. She liked it when I called her Mrs. Kent Truehl. It affirmed our oneness, I suppose. I liked her maiden name—Tanner. When I was asking God if Josephine was to be my wife, I got Romans 15:6 as my guidance, "That together you may with one voice glorify the God and Father of our Lord Jesus Christ" (NRSV). That was a powerful verse for me. But as I sought further assurance, God confirmed she was the one for me when I read the phrase "the tanner who lives by the sea."

Acts 10:32 is about the apostle Peter going to the house of Simon the tanner, but to me it was about the Tanner (Josephine) who lived in Adelaide, South Australia (by the sea). That, however, was eighteen months ago. Right now I needed $300 to pay the rent, $300 for another airfare, and $300 for spending money while in the Amazon.

"Don't be anxious, darling," she said.

After only five months of marriage she could read my face like a book. As a rather big hint that I needed a devotional time, she handed me the Book as she left the bedroom. I didn't want to fret over money, but I couldn't help it. My mind just kept going there. Josephine, on the other hand, projected a confidence that money would be there when it was needed. Maybe she had more faith than I did. Or maybe her privileged upbringing influenced her perspective. I don't know. Despite our different backgrounds, we both shared a culture of hard work and economy. My dad epitomized those characteristics. He was a union truck driver who believed no real man should ask for a handout. Josephine's father, John Tanner, had similar views.

As a newlywed couple we moved to the US Center for World Mission in California. Here we joined the team that set up a branch of YWAM Los Angeles. I knew I could not call my dad, or Josephine's dad, to ask for money, since they both were opposed to my choice of income generation. Nothing I could imagine, or even dream of, would produce the $900 I needed.

After lunch I checked our bank balance; still zero. Arriving home after going to the bank, my keenly perceptive wife sensed my melancholy. I grabbed a glass of water and sat down. Josephine came close for a hug. I informed her there had been no deposits, and that I was thinking that the trip was off and we would lose the $900 airfare.

"How can you think that?" she asserted. "God has never spoken so clearly as He has about this trip!"

"I know, but we need to pay our rent before five o'clock and we have zero money."

"Well, let's go check the mail," she said.

Our last chance for seeing miracle money was the YWAM mailbox, so we walked together to the US Center. Sorting through the stack of mail, we found one letter from Minnesota, addressed to us in beautiful handwriting.

"It's from Todd and Terry Owens," Josephine said.

I had worked part-time for Todd for two years during college. Josephine had met Todd and Terry for the first time only six weeks earlier, at our Minnesota wedding reception.

"Do you remember them?" I asked.

"Of course I do," she said, opening the envelope.

Josephine unfolded a single sheet of light-gray stationery, then cupped her hand over her mouth to keep from screaming in the US Center lobby. I grabbed the letter and saw a check for $915.37. Josephine bolted for the lobby doors. I knew she couldn't contain herself. I was right behind her as she swung the door wide and let out a scream of elation. I jumped up and down in the grass, punching my fist in victory and yelling, "God, you're amazing!"

Josephine kept right on running, leaping down the sidewalk toward home. By the time I caught up with her, we were yelling and laughing simultaneously, "Thank you, God! Thank you, God!"

Once home I looked at the check again. "What a weird amount! Nine hundred and fifteen dollars and thirty-seven cents."

"Read the letter, read the letter," Josephine pressed.

I took a deep calming breath then began:

Dear Kent and Josephine,

We enjoyed so very much seeing you both at your open house and hearing about your work with YWAM. As we drove home that day, we bubbled over with joy over the fact that we know you, Kent, and have gotten to meet you, Josephine. Two things we wished though—one was that we could have spent more time with you, and the other that we could send you support in some way. We ended it with, "We'll have to pray about it." Well, we did pray.

A couple weeks ago—and much to our shock—the government sent us the interest on tax money we should have claimed six years ago. Can you believe it? We couldn't! It didn't take long for us to realize that God had let that money pass through our fingers for a special purpose. You came to our minds. I know you guys know this—but this money is not from us, but from the Lord. Cash this check praising Him! And we will too! (The check is for such a strange amount, because that's the exact amount that came to us.)

The next day we showed Todd and Nancy Kunkler the check. We did the same with Calvin, who drove us to the bank so we could deposit it. And just as Todd and Terry requested, we cashed the check praising Him! Calvin then drove us to the travel agent, where I bought the Miami ticket. On the way home we put a special thank-you card in the mail, addressed to Todd and Terry Owens, and then paid our rent.

One week later I boarded the flight with $300 spending money in my pocket. Then, generous husband that I am, I left Josephine with the remaining balance to live on for the rest of August—$15.37.

God brought me from discouragement to direction in a single day. In the process He taught me that He, not I, was Josephine's provider. Also getting the same scripture in Mark 14, and then seeing God provide the exact amount at the last minute, gave us enduring confirmation that God not only spoke, but that he really had called us to the Amazon.

I SLID from my hammock groggy from the combination of thinking, praying, and napping. It was now early evening, so it was cool enough to be on the metal sun deck. There, Gerson joined me and recounted his short conversation with the grandpa from the floating raft.

"Most Ribeirinhos would become Christians if only there was somebody to talk to them," he said.

I pondered this as dusk gave way to darkness. Could it be as easy as that—just talking to people? I concluded there were big challenges: language, culture, and the universal resistance to change—just to name a few. But then I remembered what Gerson had said about the numerous mission agencies reaching tribal peoples, while only one sent workers to the estimated one million River People. Such an imbalance of missionaries seemed unfair.

Gerson said we would arrive in Tapauá, for the second time, sometime in the night and that I would be able to call home no matter how long we had to wait. I was looking forward to speaking with Josephine. But what would I tell her? I couldn't possibly recount in one phone call everything that had happened.

Reaching an unreached people group and planting an indigenous church among them was our hope and aspiration as missionaries. Was I ready to declare that the River People were the group we would focus our lives and efforts upon?

THIRTEEN

Ready or Not

AFTER hearing the relentless roar for days, the sudden near-silence of an idling engine woke me up out of the deepest sleep. Voices and clattering sounds indicated we were docking in Tapauá. Surely it was the wee hours of the night. I drifted back to sleep as sounds from outside merged into a strange dream. In it I saw the grandpa from the floating raft. His toothless laugh morphed into the roar of a giant grizzly bear whose long yellow claws were now shaking me with the intent of eating me for breakfast . . . "Aargh!" I screamed and sat bolt upright.

"Whoa, dude, calm down," Calvin said.

Calvin had been shaking me awake and telling me it was time for breakfast. He left the room under the wheelhouse, moving toward the smell of coffee. After realizing where I was, and what just happened, I got out of my hammock and walked zombielike toward the rich aroma of Brazilian coffee.

After breakfast, members of the American team, one by one, began piling themselves and their stuff back onto the boat. Captain Joe was doing engine maintenance, so it was a good time to call home. At TeleAmazon Gerson went straight to the desk and came back with bad news—a call to the United States was over three dollars per minute. My hope of a long catch-up with Josephine was dashed, as my money would not last long.

Josephine answered. Her joyful voice was masqueraded by electronic characteristics. I greeted her and explained we were talking on a radio. Immediately she said, "I want to share something with you. I have been so impressed by God to start having children that I embroidered a baby girl's dress!"

Here I was, calling her from the middle of the Amazon jungle, all set to tell her that I thought I was going to die in the tribe, and she starts talking babies.

"What?" I said. Not because I did not hear her. It was an involuntary response to surprise.

Josephine, on the other hand, thought I did not hear her, so she yelled into the phone slowly, "Honey, can we please have a baby?"

I was at a complete loss as to how to respond, so I asked, "Are you serious?" This bought me time to think through the implications of having a child.

Before we were married, we had talked about having four children, just like the families of two girls and two boys we each had grown up in. Since being married, however, we hadn't discussed the matter. I wasn't sure I was ready to be a father. My mind made a list of all the cultural expectations around having children: we should be settled, preferably in a nice house; we should have a steady income; we should have a long-term plan, or at least know the general direction. I didn't stack up on any of these points. But then my heart intervened—I loved children, and I had always wanted to have them. My spirit rose up in faith, and before I knew what I was doing I said, "Yes!"

"Oh, I am so excited!" And she went on talking exuberantly.

I only comprehended about half of what Josephine said, but I loved the sound of her joyfulness. I sat smiling on the other end of the phone thinking through the implications. Saying yes to having a baby seemed a faith step as extreme as this Amazon trip.

Somewhere in that torrent of talk she told how a friend of mine from high school had called. He had never called us before, but after finding out Josephine had only $15.37 for the whole month he sent her a check for $200, which arrived on her birthday. This was another amazing affirmation that God was my wife's provider, not I, even for special things like her birthday.

I finally had to stop Josephine from talking, because I feared going broke. I explained we would miss our flight and get home some days later than planned. After a long, lovey-dovey good-bye, I hung up. I had told Josephine nothing about the long trip, the jungle hike, about thinking I was going to die in the Suruwahá, or about the River People. All would have to wait.

Three more days downstream and we were back in Manaus. Everyone went their separate ways, leaving Todd, Calvin, and me in a decaying hotel near the old port with nothing to do but wait for our flight and process our experience. The hike and the encounter with the primitive Suruwahá tribe had required more of us physically, spiritually, and emotionally than any of us imagined. But, praise God, we made it. I was so glad I had come on this scouting trip. I had to go in order to know. Only here could God reveal to me what was really required to reach the unreached people of the world.

PART THREE

Her Home, My Home, Our Home

We have left everything to follow you!
What then will there be for us?

MATTHEW 19:27

Our Future

A R R I V I N G home, I swept Josephine into my arms. She made me feel centered again. After a meal and a shower back in our place at the US Center for World Mission, we both were too tired to talk.

The next morning, as Josephine made a pot of tea, she asked, "What did God show you while in Brazil?"

I had observed in our few months of marriage that Josephine is such a people-focused individual that she only wanted to hear about me, not about facts and things unknown to her.

"Well, when I was asked to pray if I should hike in to the Suruwahá, I became fearful of dying again. But, in addition to the verse we got in Mark 14, this time God gave me Psalm 56, 'In God I trust; I will not be afraid. What can mortal man do to me?'"

"I prayed for your protection every day," Josephine said.

"Thanks, we certainly needed it, because before noon on the second day of the hike I thought Calvin was going to die. Then, about six hours later, I thought we were all going to die. A Suruwahá warrior shot an arrow at Gerson and Todd."

Josephine's eyes widened and her hand instinctively covered her mouth.

"We now know he did not shoot to kill, but for a moment I thought I was going to die."

"Oh sweetheart . . ."

"But once he saw Bráulia, he worked things out. And then he thought it was hilarious that he'd scared us to death."

For more than an hour I recounted thoughts, feelings, and stories of the trip. I ended up discussing at length each option: starting a YWAM base in Manaus, working with Ribeirinhos, or working in a tribal group. The facts of each option poured forth thick and fast, as I forgot she only wanted to hear about me. Josephine soon lost interest and disappeared into the kitchen, leaving me alone in my world of theoretical possibilities and talking out loud to myself.

Lunch, and a time of prayer, brought us back together. Josephine asked again, "What did God speak when you were in the Amazon?"

"God reaffirmed our calling to the Amazon, but . . ." I said thoughtfully, "I do not see us living in a tribe. I don't think it is the right fit for our gifts and talents."

Yet, after some discussion, we agreed that we strongly believed in this work and wanted to support those who work in tribes. Then we discussed Manaus. I explained the strategic value of a property on the river in Manaus, both as a ministry center to the city and as a support base to the YWAM Amazon tribal teams.

"So is it Manaus?"

When she saw my face wrinkle in uncertainty, she quickly asked, "Or is it something else?"

"Well, Gerson said most Ribeirinhos would become Christians if only there was someone to talk to them. He said there is only one mission working among more than a million of them. Those two comments really pierced my heart."

"Is it the Ribeirinhos then?" Josephine inquired.

"Yes, I am thinking it is. Getting to some Ribeirinho communities and living among them can be just as challenging as getting to and living among a tribe," I said.

"It's exciting they are open to the gospel, but heartbreaking that almost nobody is going to them," Josephine mused.

"I think YWAM Amazon and YWAM LA could change that," I said in faith. "Maybe we should pioneer YWAM Manaus first, and then go to the Ribeirinhos."

That statement seemed right the moment it came out of my mouth. I continued this thought by describing Manaus as strategic to the success of Youth With A Mission reaching tribal groups and the River People. Missionaries working in the region needed a place to come and go from, a place of preparation and supply. A permanent YWAM base needed to be on the river so riverboats could be harbored and maintained.

Starting YWAM Manaus, supporting tribal work, and reaching the River People—our calling was not one or the other—it was all three! Our future suddenly made perfect sense.

Josephine and I wanted to be like the apostle Paul and not build on another man's foundation. We had been asking God for an unreached people group according to Psalm 2:8, "Ask of me, and I will make the nations your inheritance."

We asked. And God, in his faithfulness, was giving us the River People of the Amazon.

FIFTEEN

Australia

WE enrolled as students in YWAM Pasadena's church-planting course; however, it was canceled for lack of students, so we joined a "Night of Missions" national tour. In one month our team crossed North America in a van, promoting missions in numerous cities. While in Corning, New York, Josephine's father surprised us with a phone call. Somehow he was able to track down the family we were staying with. After the initial pleasantries, I overheard him say, "Josephine, dear, you need to come home quickly. Your mother is in a bad way."

We immediately returned to LA. Only a few months earlier Josephine's mother, June, had discovered lumps in her neck. We heard then that the diagnosis was cancer, but we were shocked to hear it had now spread to her lungs and she was on oxygen. It took several days to book flights, get me a visa, and pack up. Then mechanical difficulties grounded our flight in Honolulu.

"Isn't there something we can do to get there sooner?" Josephine pleaded.

The airline staff were sympathetic, "We're very sorry, ma'am, but there's nothing we can do until another plane arrives from the mainland."

After we'd waited thirty-six frustrating hours, our flight once again resumed. Then, about midway to Australia, Josephine began sobbing, overwhelmed with grief. When we arrived in Adelaide some hours later, we were met by her father who told it to us straight. "Josephine, my dear, your mother passed away in the night."

Josephine collapsed into her father's arms and cried tears of sadness and regret.

Only ten months earlier, preparing for our wedding, we'd stayed in June's home. We were now in her house again and the memory of her was everywhere. In our grief we questioned God. "Why did our plane break down? Why did we miss seeing her and saying our final good-bye?" While wrestling with these questions, we realized that the overwhelming grief Josephine experienced on the plane was the very time her mother died. God had been preparing Josephine for this heartbreak.

Josephine's sister and two brothers kindly took charge and gave us direction in what to do. For the next six weeks everyone juggled work commitments to get her house ready for sale. I found work in automotive upholstery, and Josephine did nursing. By mid-December the house was put up for sale. Through friends we were offered a small urban cottage rent-free. In spite of the kindness of a borrowed home and borrowed things, it was a melancholy first Christmas.

Early in the New Year, our sadness was given a welcome boost of joy with the news that our first child was on the way. Josephine took great delight in telling everyone of her pregnancy. A few days later, we attended a Christian convention where a speaker spoke on prayer. I was so impressed with his message that I bought his book and set aside the whole next morning to read it. On the second page I was so taken by one sentence that I stopped reading. It said, "Before He entered His public ministry, He spent time with the Father in prayer."[3] When I looked up this reference in chapter 1 of Mark, it was about Jesus fasting for forty days in the desert before returning to his hometown and announcing his public ministry.

I thought of fasting forty days, which was not natural for me, as I had purposely avoided fasting. Nevertheless, I could not get that challenging thought out of my mind. I read, and reread, those portions of Scripture until I admitted God was speaking that I should fast and pray forty days before commencing our public ministry.

As missionaries preparing to go to the Amazon, we had a number of commitments—many of them weekend barbecues or evening meals in homes. Not eating during those events could be perceived as antisocial. I also fretted because I had never fasted more than three days. Then I studied the calendar and counted out five working days, skipping the weekends, over eight weeks. I finalized my commitment to the Lord: To fast and pray each morning for forty weekdays to lay a spiritual foundation for our ministry in the Amazon.

Each weekday I went to a local Bible college and prayed all morning. After twenty days, my journal was filled with thoughts and Bible verses, which confirmed we were to do the same three things Jesus did before he began his public ministry. First, Jesus left the desert; then he announced his public ministry in his hometown; then Jesus moved to the town of Capernaum, which became his base for public ministry. For me, these three things meant we were to leave the desert state of South Australia. Next we would announce our ministry in my hometown of Fridley, Minnesota. Then we would move to the town that would become our base for public ministry—Manaus, Amazonas, Brazil.

Additionally, God had been speaking to me about the importance of spiritual warfare from the book of Daniel. I sensed we were to inaugurate the ministry of YWAM Manaus with twenty-one days of spiritual warfare and call it Operation Daniel. I also felt it should begin one year from today—February 1. It was exciting to receive abundant and detailed direction from God.

I shared everything with Josephine. Then for the remaining twenty days we prayerfully considered each implication. The first implication meant leaving Adelaide soon. I was sensing we were to return to LA quickly to begin the daunting challenge of inaugurating YWAM Manaus in just twelve months, but Josephine had her heart set on having our first baby in her hometown.

"Couldn't we stay and have the baby here?"

It made so much sense to have our first baby in Adelaide, surrounded by family and friends, especially since Australia's national health assistance would cover all medical costs. Having a baby in America, without health insurance, would cost thousands for a normal delivery and tens of thousands if there were complications. This seemed liked irresponsibility, not faith.

Nevertheless, despite our genuine disappointment at not having our baby in Adelaide, God reaffirmed we should do the same three things Jesus did, including leaving the desert shortly after completing forty days of prayer and fasting. By the time we left Adelaide, there were seven groups committed to praying for us regularly. Plus our friend Anthea began serving as a secretary on our behalf.

Tom Hallas, Director of YWAM Australia, invited us to national leadership meetings in Canberra the first week of March. So we set March 9, our first anniversary, as the date to leave Australia. On the last day of the meetings Tom adopted us into YWAM Australia, spoke prophetically over us, then commissioned us to Brazil all in one prayer.

On March 8 we caught a ride to Sydney. However, only forty minutes out of Canberra, the car's hot light came on. To prevent overheating, the driver detoured into YWAM Goulburn, where a mechanic diagnosed the problem.

"It won't take long to fix, but I can't get the part until Monday," he told us.

"Oh no!" I replied. "We are booked on a flight back to America tomorrow."

We tracked down the receptionist, who unlocked the YWAM office so I could try to find another way to Sydney. Just then the phone rang. The receptionist answered, even though the office was always closed on Saturdays. After a few moments the receptionist handed me the phone and said, "I think it's for you."

"Who would be calling me? No one even knows I'm here . . . Hello?"

"G'day. My name is Bruce Ferguson. I am driving to Sydney and I felt from the Lord to call YWAM to see if anyone needed a ride."

"Really? My wife and I need a ride."

"Very good then, I will be there in five minutes."

"I can't believe what happened," I told the receptionist. "We just got a ride to Sydney!"

I ran to tell Josephine that we needed to wheel our suitcases out front. Before I could recount what had happened, an immaculate old car pulled up and Bruce stepped out. He was a balding sixty-year-old wearing large glasses, a cardigan sweater, and a silk cravat like I'd seen in old James Bond films. He explained that since his retirement as city treasurer, he was sharing the gospel with inmates through regular visits to the Goulburn prison. This whole amazing set of circumstances made me think that this mysterious Bruce might actually be an angel.

As we climbed into the car, I whispered to Josephine, "Bruce just felt from the Lord . . . to call YWAM . . . to see if anybody needed a ride . . . to Sydney!"

Josephine did not catch my hint that he might be an angel and exclaimed, "Bruce, what a divine appointment!" Josephine asked so many questions that she and Bruce bantered the whole way into Sydney. Bruce spoke with a very Australian accent, which for some reason I thought was funny for an angel.

Bruce said he was a naval shipman. Bruce had never married. Bruce still lived in the house he grew up in. Bruce lived alone.

I was trying to determine the theological implications of angels tricking unwitting mortals about a fake life on earth when Bruce became subdued in the conversation. Soon he described a painful childhood. He told of being an alcoholic for over thirty years and leading a wasted and lonely life until about fifty years of age, when he finally met God.

As we entered Sydney traffic, Bruce offered to add us to his missionary prayer list.

"Oh, please do," Josephine said. "We will pray for you too!"

Bruce chose a hotel for us and drove straight there. Then he explained what train we should take into downtown to celebrate our first wedding anniversary at Sydney's beautiful harbor that evening.

As Bruce drove off, I remembered that angels attended to Jesus after he left the desert. "Thank you, God!" I said as I smiled at the thought that an angel had attended us as well.

SIXTEEN

Preparation and Provision

WE returned to LA from Australia in time to attend the YWAM Pasadena School of Frontier Missions. In the first weeks, the Lord spoke to us about the need for a riverboat to do church planting among the Ribeirinhos, in addition to starting YWAM Manaus and supporting YWAM Amazon Tribal Ministries.

One evening during the school Gerson came through on his way back to Brazil after traveling overseas. We relived some of the adventures and mishaps of our trip together. Gerson spoke about outreaches to tribal and Ribeirinho villages, in particular about a community on the Purus River near the town of Lábrea, Amazonas.

"Who knows, maybe we will minister in that place one day," Josephine said.

"I can't wait to see you two in Brazil—I mean, you three," Gerson said.

"The baby is due in August, so we're planning to move to Manaus in November," Josephine said.

"What do you think about inaugurating YWAM Manaus on February 1 next year?" I asked.

"That would be a perfect date," said Gerson.

On yet another evening, while in the produce section of a local supermarket, Josephine overheard a very Australian accent ask, "Hey, Silly Sally, how about a pineapple?"

"Is that an Australian accent?" Josephine asked.

"It sure is. My name is Mike and Silly Sally over there is also known as Celia."

"Oh, you're pregnant?" Josephine exclaimed, looking at Celia. "Me too!"

"I can see that," Celia said with a laugh. "You must be the same as me, six months?"

By the time we got to the cashier, Josephine knew that this Australian couple had lived in California for five years, that Mike got his PhD at Cal Tech, that Celia worked as a nurse, and that they became Christians in Los Angeles. They invited us to their house for a cup of tea, and we hit it off as friends.

We returned their kindness the next week by inviting Mike and Celia to hear John Dawson speak in our school. After the meeting, Mike explained how he and Celia were challenged in their Sunday school class to give financially to missions. They wanted to do that and felt encouragment from the Lord to support an Australian missionary.

Then Celia intervened, "We assumed we would find a missionary once we returned to Australia, but we found you, Josephine. Can we support you as our Australian missionary?"

"Of course!" Josephine exclaimed. "I feel so honored."

Josephine gave Celia a big hug and soon they were laughing and chatting.

"Thank you, Mike," I said. "Your decision is a tremendous encouragement to us."

Before the training school finished, I designed a brochure highlighting the three aspects of our ministry: to help start YWAM Manaus, to assist Tribal Ministries, and to church plant among the Ribeirinhos. I felt the brochure would help us raise more personal financial support. In this regard, my thought was to call my first two supporters—my sister Wanda and her husband David, and my good friend Dave Meissner.

First I called Dave, who was the youth director at my home church. In a conversation about announcing our ministry in my hometown and my need to raise money for a riverboat, he proposed a summerlong campaign with the suggested name Back the Boat.

"Dave, that would be awesome. Could you?"

"You bet. The youth will love it. It's good for the youth to learn about giving, plus it will really highlight missions."

After that encouragement I called my sister Wanda and asked if she could get her former gospel singing group to do a reunion concert. She was thrilled with the idea. "Leave it with me," she said. "I will get the gals together!"

We arrived in my hometown at the end of June. I had set a goal of raising $15,000 for a riverboat. To achieve this goal, and to announce our ministry, I distributed our brochure and was interviewed for two newspaper articles and a Christian radio station broadcast. I joined the youth group in the Back the Boat campaign activities, including a car wash, a variety show, and a Jam On for the Amazon rock concert.

As a father-to-be, I also attended prenatal classes with Josephine. One night the instructor suggested the County Hospital to us. I was skeptical because it was in a bad part of town. Upon visiting, however, we discovered that it was a brand-new building. The rooms and the setup were the very best that Josephine, an experienced midwife, had ever seen. She was overjoyed. Then, because of our low income, we qualified for state health assistance, which set a cap of $1,050, even if there were complications.

"Where God guides, He provides," I said.

The due date, August 7, came and went. Then on August 10, Josephine was awakened by labor pains, and at three o'clock in the morning of August 11, our first child, a beautiful baby girl, was born. We named her Sasha Bethany.

At the end of the month, youth director Dave handed me a check for $5,000, the result of the Back the Boat campaign. Then on September 7 about 450 people showed up for the Amazon Praise in Song concert that my sister and her gospel singing group put on. During intermission I announced our public ministry and that we would begin by moving to Manaus. After this an offering was taken up that came to $10,300. Together with the $5,000 from the youth group we surpassed our goal of $15,000.

As we were leaving church that exciting evening, an older lady from the congregation asked Josephine, "How can you take that sweet little baby down to the Amazon?"

Josephine stopped, and then instantly a thought popped into her mind, "She is safer in God's will than anywhere else."

I too was confident that we would be safe. We were walking in obedience to what God had spoken in prayer. First we left the desert state of South Australia, then we announced our public ministry in my home church. Money for the boat was in our hands, and prayer and financial supporters were rallying around us. Only the third and final step remained—moving to our base of public ministry, the city of Manaus.

SEVENTEEN

Moving Country and Culture

"WELCOME to Manaus, Amazonas, Brazil."

The announcement of our flight's arrival at 2:30 a.m. on November 25 stirred passengers from their sleep. Josephine and I struggled to guide our carry-on bags, the baby bag, the baby stroller, and, of course, the baby down the aisle. As we stepped onto the jetway, we instantly knew we were in the jungle. The sticky Amazon heat triggered rivulets of sweat that soaked our clothing even before we reached the terminal. Inside, each staff member looked about as awake as I felt. Standing like statues, they blocked one route so that the small crowd turned in unison like a school of fish until we arrived at immigration. We looked like the tourists our visas said we were. After a stare, a stamp, and a scribble, we were officially in Brazil.

Then I put Josephine and baby Sasha in the customs line with a baggage cart full of our baby stuff and carry-on bags before I went to get our checked items off the baggage carousel.

"Bem vindo ao Brasil!"

I looked up and saw the crooked smile of Dave Warner. He and his wife, Elizabeth, had taken the YWAM Pasadena Frontier Missions course and arrived ahead of us in Manaus.

"Dave, so good to see you," I replied.

Once out of the airport, and after the drive, it took three trips to carry our bags up the stairs into Dave and Elizabeth's small third-floor apartment. We were drenched with sweat by the time we finished. Five short hours later, over a breakfast of bread rolls and coffee strong enough to jolt anybody out of tiredness, Dave and Elizabeth announced that our first activity was to celebrate Thanksgiving.

"Are you serious?"

They knew we were not expecting an American life in Brazil, but they defended their decision by explaining it was a courtesy to the American pastor who had picked us up in the middle of the night. At exactly noon the distinctive beep of a Volkswagen van honked on the street below.

"The pastor has arrived," Elizabeth exclaimed as she led us down the stairs.

The American Thanksgiving meal was complete with turkey and all the trimmings. After introductions, our hosts seated us, served us, prayed table grace, and then startled us with a shocking question: "What on God's green earth are you doing here in this forsaken place?"

I almost choked on the marshmallow sweet potato I had just put in my mouth.

"You know America is a melting pot of Christian people, but not Brazil," the pastor said.

"Why is that?" I asked.

"The blacks of Brazil's northeast practice African voodoo, the Indians in the Amazon have witch doctors who consult evil spirits, and the Brazilians of European blood have adopted spiritism. Yet everyone calls themselves Catholics. It's spiritual chaos."

It went on all afternoon—story after story of nonsensical Brazilian laws, corrupt Brazilian politicians, and ridiculous Brazilian TV shows. Some hours later, after pumpkin pie and coffee, I asked the pastor something to the effect of "Why on God's green earth are you still here?"

"Oh, we're leaving," he said. "The missus already got the kids enrolled in school startin' the end of August, and I got me a job in the local hardware."

I was so relieved they were leaving Brazil that I couldn't help but gush encouragement on their plans. "Good for you. It seems like you are due for a furlough," I said.

"Oh, it's not a furlough," the pastor said. "We've clocked twelve years in this here backwater. That's more than you can expect of anybody."

"Sasha needs a nap," Josephine announced. Her eyes alternated between a plea for mercy and a death stare.

"We betta head outta here," I said. Somehow, I inadvertently slipped into a southern drawl when I said that, which made it sound like I was making fun of the pastor.

Dave intervened on my behalf and began departure formalities. Back in Dave and Elizabeth's apartment, we agreed that the afternoon ranked highly in what *not* to do on your first day in a foreign country.

"I don't think their theological college had cross-cultural training," Dave said.

"They have become pretty jaded with the culture over the years," Elizabeth added. But what he said about voodoo, witch doctors, and spiritism is actually pretty accurate."

"Well, all the more reason we are missionaries in Brazil," Josephine concluded.

On our second day in Manaus we moved into the house given to us to use by Luke Huber, the founder of the River People church-planting mission Project Amazon. Luke had warned us there were squatters in the house who refused to pay rent and refused leave. When we got there, the squatters said they needed a month or two to find somewhere else to live. We had carried our mountain of baggage down Dave and Elizabeth's stairs, so we certainly were not going back.

After a brief look in the house and meeting the squatters, I asked Elizabeth to translate for me. "Tell 'em we're moving in, and they can stay downstairs."

With that, we moved in. It was a simple two-bedroom, one-bathroom home that fronted onto a busy street. When we occupied the top floor, it forced the squatters to move into the basement, which was open to the weather on one side. It was awkward for two days sharing the bathroom and kitchen with total strangers, but they moved out on the third day.

According to our training, we dedicated ourselves to the Language Acquisition Made Practical (LAMP) methodology to learn Portuguese. It required a bilingual language helper, so the first thing we did was post a sign at the university that said, "If you can read this, we need your help."

The next afternoon the phone rang. On the other end of the line was Aylton, who explained that his wife had seen our sign. Josephine told him we were missionaries, to which he replied, "We too have had a beautiful experience with God." It was lovely having afternoon tea with Aylton and Antonia the next day. As they left they said, "Now our friends are your friends."

Inflation was out of control in Brazil, so the government imposed a price freeze to curb it. However, this resulted in shortages of many items, especially major appliances. We prayed for the much-needed appliances, yet after numerous trips to town over three weeks, we still had not seen one stove or refrigerator for sale. One day while down-town, Josephine checked the YWAM mailbox. In addition to Christmas cards was a letter from YWAM's founder Loren Cunningham confirm-ing he could speak at the YWAM Manaus inauguration. While read-ing this exciting news, she happened to see a truck open its back doors to unload. Inside were stoves, refrigerators, and freezers. Josephine climbed into the back of the truck, much to the protest of the workers, and chose one of each. After leaving a friend guarding them, she went inside the store, bought them, and had them delivered to our house.

Josephine and I did language study every day, including going into the neighborhood to use the phrases we learned. We made dozens of friendships in a few weeks, all within walking distance of our house. I met a man who had stockpiled washing machines after the price freeze and sold them out of his garage. After hand-washing diapers for a month, I decided paying a premium was worth every penny. So I bought one to surprise Josephine for Christmas.

We were expecting to celebrate Christmas quietly and alone, so we were thrilled when a family on our language acquisition route invited us to their home for Christmas Eve. It validated the philosophy of going into local communities upon arrival in a new country and confirmed that language learning was an excellent way to make friendships.

People on our language route would smile or laugh as we spoke our short and simple Portuguese phrases. This is a common language learning experience. I discovered, however, that people were not laughing with me, but at me, because of my name. Saying *Kent* in Portuguese is pronounced Kent-chee, just like the Brazilian word *quente,* meaning "hot." Unfortunately, the word *hot* had sexual connotations, which meant I was walking through the neighborhoods saying, "Hi, I'm 'hot.' What's your name?"

Because of this, I decided to choose a Brazilian name. Our book of baby names informed me that the root meaning of Kent is "white." When I met the pastor of the church that offered to host the inauguration of YWAM Manaus, I asked him what his name, Caio, meant.

"*Caio* is just a name," he said. "But the root is from the Portuguese verb *caiar,* which means 'to paint white.'"

"White, just like my name," I said.

Then I explained my name dilemma. He laughed so hard that he became as red in the face as I was from embarrassment.

"Do you have an objection to me adopting your name?" I finally asked. "Only I will spell my name with a K—Kaio."

"Of course not, Misionário Kaio." Then he laughed again. "White Missionary . . . it definitely suits you!"

EIGHTEEN

First Steps and Stumbles

THE annual conference for YWAM Amazon staff was held in Belém each January. As it was our first conference, we were looking forward to meeting all our new partners in ministry, and of course everyone was expecting us. It would be a key time of prayer and discussion about the partnership between YWAM Los Angeles and YWAM Belém.

We bought a flight that included a two-day stopover in the town midway between Manaus and Belém where Project Amazon was based. We wanted to see their ministry and thank Luke Huber for the rent-free house in Manaus.

"Luke, please join us for the inauguration of YWAM Manaus. I have a room in a nice house you can stay in."

"Oh really?" he said with a wry smile. "I'll come."

"Thank you for the generous use of the house," Josephine said.

"Not at all. I should be thanking you for evicting the squatters without involving the police or the renter's tribunal. I haven't been able to get them out for over a year!"

After a tour of Project Amazon and its new riverboat we bumped into Captain Joe and Marjory. "What are you doing here? I thought we'd see you at the YWAM conference," I said.

"We left YWAM and joined Project Amazon. I am now captain of that big nice boat you just had a tour of," Joe said. He was obviously very happy about this.

After introducing Josephine and Sasha, we drank tea and had fun retelling stories from the trip to the Suruwahá.

At the airport, to continue our journey onward to Belém, check-in staff told us that we were not on the flight.

"How can we not be on the flight? I have fully paid tickets in my hand," I said.

"Did you confirm by calling the airline twenty-four hours in advance?"

"We flew from Manaus to here, using half our ticket, isn't that confirmation?"

"I am sorry. If you did not call to confirm, your seats have been given away." Then, looking right past me, she said, "Next customer."

We stood dumbfounded with tickets in one hand and our baby in the other. The next day at the airport we put our names on the standby list, and the next day . . . and the next. Right in the middle of an emotional conundrum, thinking, *I can't believe this is happening*, I realized that our flight back home was a direct flight from Belém, which meant we did not have a reservation from the city we were in to get home. In a panic I rushed to the airline counter to change our tickets.

"I'm sorry, there are no seats available," was the expected but dreaded reply. Just then the clock must have passed the magical twenty-four-hours-before-tomorrow's-flight moment, because one seat on tomorrow's full flight suddenly became available.

"I'll take it!"

I got Josephine and Sasha on that flight to Manaus, and with the refund from my ticket I bought passage on a boat, a three-day trip. I was relieved to finally get home to Manaus but so disappointed to miss our first YWAM Amazon gathering. We hoped our message of apology to Gerson had gotten through.

I had been home only a few days when a tall, fair-skinned girl clapped her hands at our front window calling out "JOCUM."

"Yes, we are JOCUM," Josephine responded as she moved quickly to the front window.

JOCUM is the Portuguese acronym for Youth With A Mission. But since we had no sign, we had no idea how she knew who we were. I joined Josephine at the front window and saw an even taller man standing off to the side guarding their backpacks. They looked like European backpackers. After inviting them in, through charades and a confusing mix of English and Portuguese, we worked out that they were not European trekkers who'd confused Youth With A Mission with a youth hostel. Rather they were YWAM Amazon staff who had just flown in from Belém.

Daniel and Fátima stayed in the guest room for some days. Fátima taught Josephine Portuguese and helped with Sasha and in the kitchen. Daniel went into the city each morning and returned by taxi each afternoon with more shopping than he could carry. Our empty garage quickly had a large pile of gas bottles and boxes of supplies sufficient for them to stay and live in a tribe for the rest of the year.

Then, as unexpectedly as they had arrived, they announced they would leave in the morning. They explained that the *São Mateus* had traveled from Belém and was now in the Manaus port. The next morning a VW van showed up to transport them and their gear to the YWAM boat. We enjoyed showing hospitality and felt satisfied contributing in a small way to our colleagues' missionary tasks.

Seeing a spare seat in the van, I decided to go along to the port. A young YWAMer named Chico now was captain of the *São Mateus*. Also on board were Bráulia, Hulda, and a Japanese Brazilian named Suzuki. These three were returning to work with the Suruwahá. There was also a black girl from Rio named Márcia who seemed too stylish and womanly to be leading two guys in search of a lost tribe called the Arimadi. Daniel and Fátima were going to the Baniwá tribe, while two guys named Paulo and Jorge would do community development work among the Ribeirinhos. All were working in difficult jungle settings. I was amazed that these twenty-somethings like myself were doing such technical, demanding, and audacious tribal and community development work. I felt proud being JOCUM as I waved good-bye.

Later that day our phone rang. It was Anabel from Belém. "I was wondering if I could come and stay," she said.

"Of course, Anabel. It would be nice to see you again."

"I am leading a DTS outreach and actually was wondering if we could all stay with you."

"When would you come?" I asked.

"Now," she said.

"You mean today?"

"Yes, we arrived yesterday from Belém on the *São Mateus*."

"I just visited the boat this morning. How many of you are there?"

"Seven—five girls and two guys."

"I have one guest room, Anabel, which is hardly enough room for seven, and I will need that room in a little over a week for Operation Daniel guests."

I thought that would end the conversation.

"We don't need the guest room," she countered. "The two guys can sleep in the basement, and us five girls can sleep on the floor in the front room."

"Seriously, Anabel? You arrived here on outreach with no place arranged for the team to stay? You are from Manaus, so certainly you have other options like your church or your family?"

"Of course I have options, but as JOCUM you are family—so we should stay with you."

"Anabel, I am too busy organizing Operation Daniel to host a team of seven right now. Please pursue your other options."

The next morning the phone rang again. I was surprised to hear Pari Rickard's voice. Josephine and I knew him from the US Center for World Mission. Now he was the director of a Mercy Ships vessel.

"Hey, Kent, can I come and visit you in the jungle?"

"You're joking, right?

"Not at all. I need to do advance work for the ship."

"You mean you want to bring the ship here to Manaus?"

"Absolutely, that's what we felt in prayer. From Florida to Belém, then up the Amazon to Manaus."

"Wow. That would be amazing! When would you come?"

"I want to come next week, but the ship would come for five days in May."

"This will be awesome, Pari. The ship will bring more publicity in five days than what anybody could do in five years. Please come."

I was confident we were entering a season of blessing. Josephine confirmed that with an unexpected announcement: "Our first two children are going to be eleven months apart. I'm pregnant again!"

With that news, Operation Daniel began. Besides the DTS from Belém led by Anabel, there was a Summer of Service team from Brazil, a church team from California, a few from my home church, plus a team from YWAM Los Angeles that included Todd and Calvin—fifty-four people in total. Jim Stier, the founder of YWAM Brazil, translated for me as I explained how one year ago, during fasting and prayer, I had sensed God's direction to inaugurate the ministry of YWAM Manaus with twenty-one days of spiritual warfare. We spent each morning in prayer and worship followed by teaching by Jim Stier. In the afternoons and evenings, teams did street evangelism and ministered in churches.

In the second week Gerson and Alcír came to lead the training, replacing Jim. Luke Huber of Project Amazon also came, as promised. One night in the front room he and Gerson talked, and I could tell that the tone was tense. As I strained to listen, I heard my name, and that of Joe and Marjory, mentioned more than once.

The formal inauguration of YWAM Manaus with Loren Cunningham took place Saturday, February 14. That morning the phone rang. It was Loren calling from an airport in the south of Brazil. "I cannot get to Manaus," Loren said apologetically. "I have been bumped off my flight, apparently for not confirming with the airline twenty-four hours in advance."

"Oh no," I moaned, unable to contain my disappointment.

"I am so sorry," Loren replied.

Then, with more self-control, I said, "I do understand, Loren. The same thing happened to me recently. Thank you for letting me know."

Then, over the phone, Loren prayed for the inauguration of YWAM Manaus.

Because Loren could not come, Todd Kunkler preached, translated by Gerson. Then together, he and Gerson officially inaugurated YWAM Manaus. The next morning Gerson brought me, instead of Loren Cunningham, to meet the governor of the state of Amazonas at his private residence. We explained YWAM to the governor and the purpose of YWAM Manaus. We invited him to attend the dignitary's reception on board the Mercy Ship vessel in May. And as Pari requested, we petitioned for a waiver of dock fees for the duration of the ship's visit.

After this meeting, we returned home, where Alcír was waiting for us. For a number of minutes he rambled on about how he and I were not just colleagues who traded favors, nor were we "partners" who shared mutual responsibilities. I wasn't sure what he was trying to say, but I could sense something was wrong. Finally I asked, "What's up Alcír?"

This brought a long pause. "YWAM Amazon is family. And when family is in town, you drop everything and receive them. You don't say 'there is no room' or 'we are too busy.'"

He was obviously referring to Anabel and her team. "You are right, Alcír." I confessed without hesitation.

"Forgive me for being direct," Alcír continued. "But you cannot care more about your job than your family."

"OK, I get it. I am very sorry about that. Please forgive me."

Then Gerson turned to me. "We only have one staff conference a year and you cannot afford to miss it."

"The airline bumped us, just like they did to Loren."

"As soon as Operation Daniel is finished, I want you and Josephine to give this house back to Project Amazon and move to Belém. I want you to live on the base with us like family."

I was stunned. Unilateral decisions were not what I was expecting from a ministry partnership. Defiance welled up in my mind, creating a list of reasons for doing otherwise.

"I have appointed Zezinho and Fran interim directors of YWAM Manaus," Gerson said.

My American concept of partnership, which was nothing like the Brazilian concept of family, had clearly caused pain. I reminded myself that YWAM Manaus was Gerson's vision, which I had offered to help him with, so I really had no reason to be angry or defiant. Plus, I deeply respected him. I decided I needed to trust God in this.

Gerson and Alcír were waiting for me to say something. Just then I remembered some words of wisdom John Dawson once shared: "No man can thwart the plan of God for your life." With that in mind I said, "We'll be there within a month."

NINETEEN

Gaining and Losing

AYLTON, who helped me organize Operation Daniel and get that meeting with the governor, helped me again by finding a large four-bedroom house to rent. Zezinho and Fran, the interim leaders of YWAM Manaus, moved in the same day as us. YWAM would use our furniture and other household belongings while we were in Belém.

"Exchanging a rent-free house on the bus line and close to everything for a rental property off the beaten track is an unexpected change," I said grumpily.

Josephine frowned at my sarcasm. "Gerson just wants YWAMers received by JOCUM not by Project Amazon or any other American mission."

We arrived in Belém within a month and were warmly welcomed. We set to work making friends and serving the base. We lived in a small room under the roof of the main building and shared a bathroom, kitchenette, and a large open area with others. We soon learned Brazilians love community life. The open area buzzed as a gathering place for parties, singing, and prayer. Sasha delighted everyone as she scurried around the wooden floor in her baby walker.

Josephine and I worked in the kitchen and looked after preschool children. We also did paperwork for our Brazilian permanent residency visas. Brazilian immigration informed us that visas took about six months and were issued only outside of Brazil. The last thing we wanted to do was move again, but it seemed we had no choice. As we prayed, we felt Australia was the location to wait for our visas and have our second child.

The M/V *Good Samaritan* arrived in Belém in early May. Josephine and I gave Pari and Diane big hugs and welcomed them and their crew to Brazil.

"Welcome to Belém, the gateway to the Amazon," Gerson said. "Thank you for coming."

"We are thrilled to be here," Pari said.

Virtually everyone at the base assisted in the Mercy Ships outreach. Over the next week, hundreds of people received free medical care and heard the gospel message. Gerson was delighted. Since our six-month tourist visas were expiring and our tickets out of the country were from Manaus, Pari and Gerson authorized us to travel on board, up the Amazon from Belém to Manaus. Sasha took her first steps while in our small cabin on board.

In Manaus, the ship brought more exposure to YWAM than we could have had in years. It was the first Christian medical vessel to visit the city, so it attracted citywide attention. As was hoped, hundreds of people visited the ship each day and learned about YWAM Manaus. Once again the teams worked tirelessly, doing seminars, receptions, and outreaches, with many receiving both the gospel and medical or dental care.

After a week, Josephine and I said good-bye to Pari and Diane and the ship's crew as the ship began its journey back to the United States via Belém. We also said good-bye to Anabel, Alcír, and Gerson, thanking them for their orientation, support, and guidance during our first six months in Brazil. A few days later we flew to Australia.

Arriving back in Adelaide after a two-hemisphere, three-continent journey, we felt our strength ebb away like a retreating tide. It wasn't only from jet lag and forty hours of travel. We were suffering a physical, emotional, and spiritual backwash from six months of the relentless intensity of a new country, culture, and language. After finding a small rental unit, we barely had the wherewithal to move again. Josephine's father helped us. As he did, he said, "Rent money is drain money, Josephine. It is a buyer's market; now is the time to buy."

We had just received an inheritance from the sale of Josephine's mother's house. With this money invested in shares, the idea of buying a house did not seem far-fetched, so we started looking and praying.

On Sunday, July 12, we celebrated my birthday with lunch at Josephine's father's house. Josephine had been experiencing labor pains since early that morning, which intensified through church and lunch. As she gasped through another strong contraction, she said, "I'm sorry, darling, but I think we have to cut short your birthday party."

"That's fine with me. It's going to be an even more special birthday for me."

We rushed to the hospital and only three hours later a petite baby girl was born. We named her Chloe Christiana. She was beautiful. Once again we were overcome by the awe-inspiring miracle of birth, as well as the responsibility we now carried in our arms.

About one month later we felt physically, emotionally, and spiritually reinvigorated, and that was when our permanent residency visas for Brazil arrived. As I opened our passports, I was prompted by God to make decisions about Brazil based on the long term, not on the short term. These two promptings in spirit, buying a house and making long-term decisions about Brazil, suddenly converged; we were not to buy a house in Australia, but in Brazil!

I talked to Josephine about this and we prayed together. She had given up her special wedding money for my trip to Brazil two years ago, and now I felt like I was asking her to give up her Australian inheritance for Brazil.

"What do you want to do?" I asked hesitantly.

"It's our inheritance money, darling, so it's our decision, not just mine."

After some days of prayerful consideration we talked again. Josephine was confident, "I believe we need to give all. I got Matthew 19:29, which says, "Everyone who has left houses or brothers or sisters or father or mother or children or fields for my sake will receive a hundred times as much and will inherit eternal life."

"Through prayer I felt God reconfirm that in relation to Brazil we are to make long-term decisions in every way—spiritually, emotionally, physically, and financially," I said.

With this agreement and spiritual conviction, on August 25 I went to the high-rise downtown office of our brokerage firm. A glamorous receptionist opened the heavy wooden doors and ushered me through to one of the senior brokers, who sat behind a giant desk in front of a huge window overlooking the Adelaide skyline.

"What can I do for you?" he boomed.

I plucked up my courage and replied, "I want to sell all my shares."

"How come?"

"We are moving to Brazil, and we want to buy a house when we get there."

"When will you get there?"

"In two or three months."

"First of all, we are in the midst of one of the biggest stock market runs in history. The firm is advising all clients to stay fully invested." He opened my portfolio, had a quick look, and then continued. "Your investments are in low-risk blue-chip stocks and have grown 15 percent."

My spiritual conviction was that I needed to sell everything, but I did not know how to explain this to the worldly-wise stockbroker in front of me. So I tried a rational approach.

"Yes, the investments have done very well, thanks to you. Which is why we want to sell now—quit while we are ahead, so to speak."

"You would be foolish to sell now. You would lose all potential earnings over the six months it will take you to find the right house. Don't worry, when you find a house, I will sell all the shares and wire your money where you need it."

I suddenly felt powerless, my spiritual conviction reduced to a mere trace. Maybe he was right. After all, he was the professional. As I bemoaned my tendency to acquiesce to strong personalities rather than declare what I felt or wanted, the strockbroker jolted me out of my pondering. "Is that everything for today?"

"No," I said with more courage. "I need some money now for expenses and our airfare back to Brazil."

This was the truth, but it was also a compromise. The truth was we needed some money now; the compromise was that I did not sell everything as I had sensed in my spirit to do.

Another six weeks later baby Chloe's permanent visa was issued and we flew to LA and debriefed with our YWAM leaders there. In October we went to Minnesota to visit family and raise more financial support. Not long after our arrival, I heard shocking news on TV—a 22.6 percent fall on the stock market since its peak on August 25.

"Josephine, did you hear the news? August 25 was the day I went to the brokerage firm and told them to sell everything!"

The bad news continued with phrases like "the biggest one-day fall since the Great Depression" and "a global economic meltdown." I started to panic. Seven in the evening was 10:30 a.m. in South Australia, so I decided to call the investment firm. "Why didn't I sell everything when I knew I was supposed to?"

I punched the numbers into the phone and got a recording.

"The Australian stock exchange declined 30 percent overnight. Selling shares now will lock in any losses incurred. The firm advises staying fully invested. If you still wish to speak to a personal investment advisor, please dial 1 now."

I was stunned. A 30 percent decline was a huge loss. I hung up the phone in utter dismay.

"Is it bad, sweetheart?" Josephine grimaced.

"It's worse."

I was so incensed that I had allowed that stockbroker to intimidate me. The fear of man in my life had led me down a path of compromise, which was nothing less than disobedience to what the Spirit of God had spoken into my spirit.

The markets continued to fall. By the time we returned to Manaus in late November, we had gained a few hundred dollars more in monthly support but had lost almost 40 percent of our inheritance.

TWENTY

Investing All

PUTTING that painful loss behind us, we were warmly welcomed by Mario and Jaçiara da Silva, the new leaders of YWAM Manaus. They allocated us a small room in the four-bedroom rental house we had found. The male staff and students slept in hammocks under the veranda, which doubled as the eating area and the Discipleship Training School classroom during the day. The female staff and female students each had a room, as did Mario and Jaçiara. The bedroom for Zezinho, Fran, and their newborn was the living room. There were twenty adults and three babies in the four-bedroom house.

We asked Mario and Jaçiara how we could help and what ministry opportunities or needs there might be.

"YWAM Manaus could certainly do more if we had a car," Mario said.

"Maybe we can help with that," I replied.

"Do you have a car?" Jaçiara asked with a puzzled expression.

"No, but we have been praying about getting one. Could you help us find one?"

"Sure," they replied in unison.

They scoured the classifieds and called around on our behalf and soon found a small Ford station wagon that we could buy with the remainder of our money after buying airfare back to Brazil. The couple that sold me the car had moved from São Paulo, and transferring the car title to us became a bureaucratic nightmare. It took three days to secure a temporary transfer card.

But that wasn't the end of it. A few nights later a YWAMer asked for a ride to the port.

"Sure, let's go."

We hopped into my station wagon and headed straight into the busy Saturday night traffic. I managed to find the port, but after dropping off my passenger, I mistakenly exited into a bus-only lane. A police officer saw me and blew his whistle. My heart jumped. Having a run-in with the police in a foreign country was one of my worst fears. I obediently stopped right there. But soon a long line of buses began blowing their horns because I was blocking them from moving into the city bus station. There was nowhere to go but forward, so I sped ahead to allow the buses to keep moving. I thought the cop must have been thinking I was trying to avoid arrest, but I remained calm and pulled over again. Then I realized I'd left my wallet at home.

"Oh Lord," I cried out as the policeman ran up barking commands in Portuguese. I suddenly forgot every word of Portuguese I had learned.

"*Por favor*," I pleaded. "License at *casa*."

Just then Pastor Francisco called out to me from a passing bus. We had met months earlier when he visited the M/V *Good Samaritan*.

"Help me, Pastor," I hollered.

"Stop the bus! Stop the bus!" he shouted.

It stopped abruptly and the pastor bounded out. Soon the policeman directed us into my car and, getting in with us, ordered me to drive home to get my license. The policeman had never seen anything like it, as it was an official translation of my American license. Nor had he seen a temporary transfer card, or a car with São Paulo plates. He thought everything very suspicious.

"We must go to police headquarters," he commanded. So off we drove again. Zezinho joined us, his pockets stuffed with gospel tracts. At police headquarters the captain on duty quickly approved my translated license, but he too had never seen São Paulo plates in Manaus before, or a temporary transfer card.

"I need to make some inquiries," he said and returned to his office.

Pastor Francisco and Zezinho launched into explanations of the gospel tracts to various policemen who had gathered at the counter. About thirty minutes later the businessman and his stylish wife who had sold me the car walked in.

"I am so sorry," I gushed apologetically as they entered.

"No problem," they replied.

The police captain returned to the counter and for almost half an hour it was a spectacle of debate, documents, and gospel tracts. Shortly after midnight it was finally over. Pastor Francisco was praying with a young police recruit in the corner, but everyone else was laughing and shaking hands like best friends. As for me, I received no traffic violation.

"Drive the officer to his home," the captain commanded. "His shift is over."

Back at the YWAM house, living with eighteen other adults was complicated, and Mario and Jaçiara had no role for us. They had hinted we should consider renting our own house. Some days later, just a few weeks before Christmas, we drove down the main street of a nearby residential district and discovered a beautiful house for sale. Based on the word of the Lord to make long-term decisions and invest all in Brazil, we asked the Lord about buying it. After much prayer over the next two weeks, we felt strongly that we were to step out in faith and buy, even though the house cost more than what was left of our inheritance.

At the Belém January conference, when asked about our plans for the coming year, we informed our colleagues that we were buying a house in order to do language learning every morning in our neighborhood and take Portuguese classes every afternoon. Our Brazilian coworkers were shocked by our news.

In mid-January, back in Manaus, we instructed the brokerage firm to sell and wire over everything we had. We also borrowed $3,600 to make up the shortfall, which a good friend from home provided.

The unpleasant task of moving became acutely awkward because it meant taking the fridge, freezer, washing machine, and our furniture out of the base—stuff that everybody was using. The whole situation was distressing, especially driving away in the only vehicle, our car. The look on our coworkers' faces was stone cold.

Once around the corner I said, "This is not coming across well. How can the word of the Lord be so wrong?"

"Honey, you can't say that. If God said it, then we must believe it and act on it, that's it. You have to break the fear of man off your life. You cannot let the opinions of our Brazilian colleagues, or anyone else, make decisions for us," Josephine said.

"I just don't know how to reconcile a word of the Lord that results in such a cross-cultural mess."

"Sweetie pie, there is everything right about a family having their own space and living according to their own schedule. We'll just have to work extra hard to make sure we don't become isolated from our colleagues."

"I totally agree. I have already offered to drive and help in any way. However, language learning is priority, otherwise we will be isolated forever. As missionaries, they should understand that."

"And as missionaries they would also understand that reaching the lost means not spending all your time with fellow Christians," Josephine added.

Only days after moving into our new home, our commitment to language learning and engaging the community started to pay off. I met a neighbor walking her baby in a stroller while I was outside with Sasha. Seeing that we both had girls of similar age, we introduced ourselves.

"I'm Cleide, and this is my daughter Cinthia. We live a few doors down."

"Hi, I'm Kaio, and this is my daughter Sasha."

We discovered our daughters shared the same birthday.

"They must be destined to be friends," Cleide said.

Cleide became Josephine's language helper. After some weeks she opened up in deep friendship and shared with Josephine about being in an abusive marriage. This led to numerous meaningful conversations. Her husband worked all day, then ran his own business in the evenings. The business seemed to be a place of getting drunk and partying with women, leaving Cleide to look after the five children while working full-time as a teacher.

Several times Josephine prayed with Cleide and invited her and her children to come to church with us, but on this point she continually declined.

One Sunday afternoon, however, Cleide's son came running. "Mom got burned!" he yelled in a panic.

While Josephine ran for a prescription burn cream we had brought from Australia, he described how his mom was having difficulty lighting the oven when the accumulated gas burst into flames, burning her forearms, neck, and face. We dashed to their house, and Josephine applied the cream and prayed for God to heal her. The following week, Cleide brought her children, and her husband, to church with us. They came again the next Sunday, without the husband, and on that Sunday Cleide gave her life to Christ.

As for me, I bought bread every day at the local bakery, which was owned by a talkative guy named Leonardo. He mentioned he had free time from late morning until midafternoon most days and offered to be my language helper. One Saturday afternoon Josephine and I went to pay him and his wife and daughter a social visit. When we arrived, Leonardo's wife, Val, received us solemnly. Potted plants lay smashed around the veranda, and Leonardo was passed out drunk on the sofa. Val invited us in and told us she was in the midst of packing her bags to leave.

"God can help you and Leonardo in your marriage. The gospel is good news in every area of life," we said.

It took some hours, but Josephine and I were able to persuade her to stay and give the marriage, and God, a try. The next morning when I was buying bread at the bakery, Leonardo pulled me aside and apologized. Then he asked if he and Val could accompany us to church that very evening.

Over the next few weeks Leonardo mostly asked questions about faith during our language sessions. Some months later, after many discussions, both Leonardo and Val accepted Christ during a church service. One Sunday several months later, Leonardo put a set of keys in the church offering. I would not have known about this, except I was with Leonardo for a language session when the pastor called. Leonardo explained that the keys were for a bakery property he had been unsuccessful in selling. He donated a three-story building on a main road to the church, so they could use it for a Bible school and seminary they had been praying to start.

When I told Josephine what Leonardo did, she joyfully exclaimed, "This is what it means to be missionaries. Cleide and Leonardo—their lives and their families' lives—are changed for eternity."

PART FOUR

Ministry Foundations

By the grace God has given me, I laid a foundation as an
expert builder, and someone else is building on it.

1 CORINTHIANS 3:10

TWENTY-ONE

Money and Ministry

I T was a happy year living in our family home, learning the language, and making friends with our neighbors. Sasha and Chloe played happily each day in our large backyard. They especially loved discovering fallen avocados and mangoes from under the many fruit trees. When it rained, I would park the car on the street so they could play in the tiled carport. It was also much cooler there than inside the house. One day, after the girls had been playing there, Josephine was picking up their strewn toys when she screamed. I came running. A colorful, but deadly, black and orange coral snake just slid through the carport. Together we thanked the Lord for his protection, as the girls had only just been put down for a nap.

Since my visit to the Suruwahá, Bráulia had married a Baptist Bible-college graduate from São Paulo named Reinaldo. His relaxed and witty disposition as a YWAM leader moderated Gerson's urgency and Bráulia's passionate intensity. His knack for playing the jester, and the devil's advocate, was a sharp contrast to the "special forces" culture of

YWAM Amazon. We met him for the first time in Belém, at the annual conference, where it was announced that Tribal Ministries would be put under Reinaldo and Bráulia's leadership. At their commissioning ceremony they shared their vision, which now included boats, because Mercy Ships had given an offering of $6,000 toward a riverboat that would get them to and from the Suruwahá. Afterward, Dave and Elizabeth and Josephine and I shared our interest in boats for the purpose of church planting among the River People.

"We hope to build a large boat to bring teams on outreach upriver," Dave said.

"This is much needed," Reinaldo said. "I can foresee how boats serving among the Ribeirinhos will also support tribal ministry work."

"We hope to build a boat too. We were donated money for one two years ago," I said.

"How much?" Reinaldo asked bluntly.

This caught me off guard because in my experience Brazilians were straightforward about everything except money.

"We have $15,000," I said sheepishly.

In midyear, Reinaldo and Bráulia came to Manaus. They had already spent months looking for a suitable boat in Belém, but without success, so they thought they would try Manaus.

"Wow, a luxury car," Reinaldo said as I picked them up at the airport.

"Are you talking about this? A small Ford station wagon is hardly a luxury car, Reinaldo."

"To me any car is luxury."

Bráulia could see that I did not know how to respond to him. "Stop it, Reinaldo," she said. "Don't mind him. He teases everybody."

We enjoyed each other's company and shared many laughs. It was good getting to know Reinaldo and Bráulia better. Reinaldo was funny, and a gifted communicator, but his intricate use of pun and innuendo was very difficult for us to understand cross-culturally. Josephine and I would review our interactions with him and try to determine if he was commending us or challenging us; most of the time we weren't sure either way.

One day Mario and Jaçiara came for a visit along with Reinaldo and Bráulia. As we were offering cool drinks to everyone, Reinaldo announced they'd bought a boat.

"Oh, that's great!" Josephine and I said simultaneously.

"I have even more good news," Bráulia said. "Mercy Ships contacted Gerson and will be making a second visit to the Amazon this October."

Jaçiara squeezed her eyes and fists tightly, and in her gentle voice said, "Thank you, Jesus."

"Sweet," I said loudly. "Two visits in two years—what an amazing blessing."

"The *Good Samaritan* will spend one week each in Belém and Manaus, just like last time," Bráulia concluded.

As we talked about how the first visit of the *Good Samaritan* was such a fruitful time of ministry, Reinaldo interrupted. "Stop. We have even more news."

"Really, what now?" Jaçiara asked in anticipation.

"We found a large property not far beyond the airport for a really good price."

"How much?" Mario asked.

"It is on an inlet of the Negro River with three hundred feet of river frontage. It is the perfect location for YWAM Manaus."

"What's the asking price?" Mario pressed.

"It's super inexpensive, Mario, but that's because it has no buildings or infrastructure, no electricity, phone, sewer, or water."

"Reinaldo, how much?" demanded Mario.

"Thirty thousand US dollars," Bráulia said, cutting short Reinaldo's drawn-out drama.

Everyone looked at Mario to see his reaction. His eyes were on the ceiling but his lips were moving—you could tell he was trying to calculate the currency conversion.

"It's a great price," Bráulia said. "The land is big and beautiful. Right on the river."

"That is a good price for a riverfront property, but it is still a lot of money we don't have."

"The owner wants $15,000 down and another $15,000 after thirty days," Reinaldo said.

Mario grimaced. "It's going to be hard to raise that much money so fast."

"It won't be hard. Just ask Kaio," Reinaldo blurted out. "For two years he's had $15,000 of YWAM money just sitting in his bank account!"

Everyone looked at me in astonishment. Then in unison, everyone returned their gaze back to Reinaldo to see if he was joking.

"He does! He told me so himself."

"It's for a riverboat," I defended.

"Well, your brochure has the YWAM Manaus logo on the front cover, and a picture of a tribe on the inside, so I thought maybe half the money was for YWAM Manaus and the other half was for Tribal Ministries," Reinaldo said.

I pointed out that the brochure was our personal communication announcing our intentions to help start YWAM Manaus and to assist Tribal Ministries. I also informed them that a fundraising campaign called Back the Boat had raised the money. Unfortunately, my explanation did not seem to satisfy either Reinaldo or Mario.

Reinaldo intimated it was practically immoral for $15,000 to sit in the bank for two years while ministry teams had such stark needs.

"Tell me, Reinaldo, what are the stark needs you are referring to?"

While Reinaldo was thinking, Mario asked if the money could be given, or loaned, to help buy the riverfront property.

"I don't think so," I replied.

Reinaldo finally thought of some needs. "Daniel and Fátima need a small boat and motor to get to and from the Baniwá."

"Small boats are handy for a hundred things," Mario confirmed. "I could really use one for the *São Mateus*."

"Even YWAM Belém needs a dinghy for the hospital boat they are building," Reinaldo said, and then added, "Heck, I just became the owner of a riverboat myself. I should have one too."

"How much do they cost?" I asked.

"I looked a couple months ago," Mario volunteered. "A new fifteen-foot aluminum boat with a fifteen-horsepower outboard costs over $5,000."

"So three small boats and motors would use up all the money I have. Then what would I use to do church planting among the River People?"

Neither Reinaldo nor Mario commented on my question.

Mario was confounded as to how I'd opened a bank account in the name of YWAM Manaus without his, or Gerson's, authorization.

He and Reinaldo agreed that only they, Alcír, and Gerson should be controlling YWAM finances; I was the notable omission to that list of leaders. Josephine, Jaçiara, and Bráulia brought a welcome conclusion to the conversation by bringing out some sandwiches.

A week later, Mario and Jaçiara gathered the Manaus staff to pray earnestly about purchasing the riverfront property Reinaldo and Bráulia had found. Mario contacted the four other YWAM bases in Brazil, various churches, and potential donors about helping with the purchase.

With the *Good Samaritan* coming for a second visit, we called my parents in the States so Josephine could share her idea of Redeemer Lutheran gathering some needed goods to be brought down on the ship for YWAM Amazon ministries.

"That's a good idea. People would rather give old stuff to missionaries instead of having all the work of a garage sale," Mom said.

"How is everything going to get to Florida?" Dad questioned from the phone line in the bedroom.

"I don't know. It wouldn't be that hard would it?" Josephine replied, not fully aware of US geography.

"Geeeez, it's on the other side of the country."

Hearing Dad's loud retort made Josephine look to me for help. I quickly took the phone and said, "It's just a thought, Dad. Don't worry about it. I'll ask the missions committee and see what they say. In the meanwhile, could you do me a favor and see what a fifteen-foot fishing boat and a fifteen-horsepower outboard motor costs?"

Before we called again, we got a long letter from Mom. She wrote how Dad said it wasn't even worth asking the church missions committee about donations if the donations couldn't get to the ship. Then she said that Dad had decided to take vacation time off work so they could drive the donations to Florida. She also said that Dad had found four used aluminum fishing boats for only $300 each, only 10 percent the price of a new boat in Brazil. He also found a deal on brand-new ten-horsepower outboard motors. These were about half the price of a similar engine in Manaus.

After prayer with Josephine about this, I called home and gave Dad the go-ahead to buy four used fishing boats and four new outboards, spending $6,000 of the $15,300 of boat money. Then I called my home church, which led to donations of office equipment, desks, filing cabinets, air conditioners, power tools, hand tools, mountains of dishes, pots and pans, utensils, and other kitchen items and even a few stoves and refrigerators.

The large amount of donated stuff required Dad and Mom to hire a large moving truck. After the four-day trip from Minnesota to Florida, the items were loaded onto the *Good Samaritan*. I asked Mom to label one boat and motor for the YWAM Belém hospital boat, one boat and motor for the *São Mateus*, now in Manaus with Mario and Jaçiara, one boat and motor for Daniel and Fátima of Tribal Ministries, and one boat and motor for Paulo and Jorge of Community Development Ministries.

TWENTY-TWO

Faith and Provision

IN early September Mario announced YWAM Manaus would buy the riverfront property. The small Manaus team led the way in generosity, with one couple putting their gold engagement rings in the first offering. YWAM Belém and the four other YWAM centers in Brazil also contributed significantly. It was hoped that the whole amount of $30,000 would be raised straightaway, but the economic climate in Brazil was very bad, and by mid-September only half of the money had come in. Nevertheless, after another morning-long prayer session, there was a unanimous sense among the Manaus staff that we were to step out in faith. With that, Mario and Jaçiara paid the $15,000 down payment and started the clock. This left thirty days to pay the remaining $15,000, or else we would lose our down payment and the land would go back up for sale. I had tremendous admiration for Mario and Jaçiara for taking this huge leap of faith.

The *Good Samaritan*'s second visit was just as much of a blessing as the first. All the goods donated by my church and driven to Florida by my parents were happily received—especially the four boats and motors. In spite of these blessings, the mood was subdued in Manaus. YWAM was days away from losing the property and the $15,000 down payment.

Mario summoned me as the accountant, and as a translator, to share the urgent need about the property during the *Good Samaritan*'s staff meeting. The ship director was very sympathetic and immediately took up an offering among the crew. I could see hope rising in Mario as the bucket circulated among the many foreigners in the room. After the offering, the meeting was dismissed and we went to count the money. Mario's countenance once again went dull, as the offering netted only a few hundred dollars.

Mario, being bold and feeling desperate, cornered the director and pressed him for help—even a loan. I was embarrassed by Mario's directness, but I translated exactly and faithfully. The director's reply, however, left Mario and me staggered at the colossal financial challenges Mercy Ships was facing. Being a faith ministry, they were dependent on donations just as we were. Then, to top it off, they needed much more money than we did, just to get back to America. It seemed like the last nail in our coffin. Mario and I had nowhere left to turn.

Later that morning, both Mario and I had to put aside any personal anxiety about the lack of funding in order to minister to others. I gave a seminar in the reception room to church worship leaders, followed by Mario, who gave a seminar to senior pastors. While Mario lunched with the senior pastors, I had lunch with the ship's director. Ironically his name was Kent, and he was also from Minnesota. After lunch the ship's director pulled Mario and me aside.

"Do you have a bank account in Minnesota?" he asked, looking at me.

"Yes, I do, and so does YWAM Manaus," I replied.

"One of the crew is offering a $15,000 loan from their personal account for YWAM Manaus to buy the property, but only if you can pay it back in six months."

It didn't take Mario long to say yes after I translated the offer.

The next morning I arrived at the YWAM Manaus rental property with a check for $15,000 from the YWAM Manaus account in Minnesota. Mario stood before the staff and students, check in hand, and gleefully announced God's provision and perfect timing to the cheers and gratitude of all. I too praised the Lord.

Another miraculous episode occurred only a month later. Jim Stier and a friend named John, who was nicknamed JFK, accompanied John Dawson on a visit to Manaus. After picking them up at the airport, I brought them straight out to the new YWAM property. It was hot, so we went for a swim. While I had a relaxing conversation with Jim and JFK, John finished preparing the sermon he would give later that night.

John preached a message titled "Discerning the Gates of Your City"[4] at the same church that had hosted the inauguration of YWAM Manaus eighteen months earlier. John shared the revelation God had given him about the "strong man" operating over the city of Manaus. As John described his revelation, it felt like a curtain was being drawn back from my veiled eyes, enabling me to see spiritual realities I was previously blind to. Josephine was sensing the same, nodding in agreement throughout John's message.

Back home, after Jim and JFK went off to bed, Josephine asked John if we could speak to him further. We got some drinks and found cool refuge on the tiles of the outdoor veranda.

"I can see so clearly the dominating, contentious strong man," I said. "But after discerning what the Bible calls a territorial spirit, then engaging in spiritual warfare prayer, is that all? Or is there something else we should do?"

"Taking our cities for God requires breaking spiritual strongholds," John replied. "In the offensive sense, you do this by acting in the opposite spirit. In the defensive sense, you do this by resisting the temptations these spiritual forces of darkness bring your way, such as losing heart concerning the future, becoming judgmental toward authority figures, and walking in polite but superficial relationships."

John's observations left us reeling with a mix of mind-blowing insights and palpable regrets. We poured out our hearts as to how these three temptations defined too many moments of our first two years in Brazil. After hours of sharing, discussing, prayer, and repentance we felt so released, refreshed, and empowered to continue in our calling.

As we got ready for bed, I confessed to Josephine that I had contemplated giving up because I was losing heart about our future here. Instead of seeing my struggles as against spiritual forces of evil in the heavenly realms, like it says in the Bible, I had become judgmental toward my leaders.

The next day Mario and Jaçiara took John, Jim, JFK, and me on an overnight fishing trip. Mario, Jaçiara, and I alternated in telling the brief history of YWAM Manaus while we plied the waters of the Negro River. After hearing the story of God's provision, and the unpaid private loan, JFK conferred with Jim Stier and John Dawson and offered to match up to $7,500 of money raised by YWAM Manaus. The next day our three visitors left, but JFK's incentive remained. With new hope and energy Mario sent all staff to their homes for the rest of November and December to raise funds.

A few weeks later Richard Krantz, an architect from Southern California who responded to a request in our newsletter, flew in. He spent a week in Manaus, giving his time and talents free of charge. He painted a beautiful ink and watercolor master plan of the riverfront property that showed the future facilities. The bird's-eye view gave graphic form to the vision Mario and Jaçiara had for the YWAM base.

Over the next few months I recorded the source and amount of every gift received by YWAM Manaus. When it reached $7,500, I reported this to JFK, who gave a matching gift, enabling us to repay the $15,000 loan before the due date. Money continued to come in even after the $7,500 was reached, an additional $6,000 in fact.

During our first two-year commitment we learned valuable lessons about adjusting to a culture vastly different from our own Australian and American way of life. We made significant cultural blunders, but through them God was forming our character and teaching us humility, repentance, and essentials for longevity in the Christian walk.

Significantly, the riverfront land of Gerson's vision was now a reality. The property was paid for, the master plan was complete, and YWAM boats had safe harbor. We felt a sense of closure and completion. Was it now time to do church planting among the Ribeirinhos?

TWENTY-THREE

An Invitation

THIS time the January Belém conference would be differ-ent. Our first conference was a disaster because we'd missed the whole thing when the airline bumped us off the flight. Last year was a disas-ter because our announcement of buying a home and doing language learning for the whole year had dropped like a lead balloon. This year we received compliments on our Portuguese, and everyone was amazed to hear that both of our language helpers had come to Christ.

We had a lot to be proud of this past year: our home and car served many people, my church donated many things that my parents sent down on the *Good Samaritan*, and the four boats and motors were a huge blessing to YWAM Belém, YWAM Manaus, Tribal Ministries, and Community Development Ministries. We also had a role in the pur-chase and payment of the YWAM Manaus property, in addition to get-ting the master plan organized and completed. We had a deep sense of satisfaction with this list of achievements. Most importantly, we felt accepted into the JOCUM family. If we wanted to leave now, we could do so with honor and in good conscience. However, we eagerly made a second two-year commitment in order to pioneer what we really wanted to do in the Amazon—church planting among an unreached people group.

The afternoon meetings at the Belém conference took the form of reporting. Beth and Sandra, two girls working with the Jarawara tribe, were giving a report. Since it was so hot and we did not do linguistics in a tribe, I was struggling to pay attention.

". . . a River People village . . . health care . . ."

Those words aroused me from a micro-nap. "Did you get that?" I asked Josephine.

"Get what?"

"Something about health care and the River People?"

"No, I missed that," Josephine confessed.

Afterward, we sought out Beth and Sandra, who explained that the landowner of a River People community en route to the Jarawara village had extended an open invitation to YWAM missionaries to live in their community if they would work in health care. The next day we met Afonso, the third member of Beth and Sandra's team. He informed us that the Jarawara were located within the municipality of Lábrea, the very town Gerson had mentioned to us almost three years before, while training in Los Angeles. This got our attention, because when Gerson had spoken about Lábrea, Josephine replied something to the effect that we might minister there one day. I'd thought her comment was way out there, but now it seemed very prophetic. After an affirming and stimulating discussion we arranged to visit this River People community, called Samaúma.

Returning home to Manaus, we learned that Josephine was pregnant with our third child. This added to our excitement and hope for the year. In mid-February, Josephine and I flew to Lábrea for five days, leaving our girls with a live-in babysitter we knew through our church.

Afonso met us at the Lábrea airport and brought us to a Dutch mission that sat at the junction of the airport road and the Transamazon Highway. The Transamazon looked like a mud track unsuitable for vehicle travel. Lábrea also looked rather unsuitable. It seemed to lack coherence and a sense of identity. Although a town of 30,000 people, there was no local radio or newspaper, no big business, just a few self-sustaining small businesses and only about eight hundred evangelicals in five churches. The level of poverty, the lack of industry and civil services, and the lack of basic infrastructure was appalling. Talking to the people, it became apparent that the majority of the population did not really want to live Lábrea. Afonso said the Ribeirinhos, and an increasing number of tribal people, were almost forced to abandon their roots in the rural interior in order to access health care. In other words, they were not trying their luck in the city in an aspirational sense; they came because they had to.

The whole next day was spent traveling up the Purus River beyond Lábrea. There were no churches in any of the communities we passed. Afonso told us there was only one Ribeirinho church in the 220 rural villages within the municipality of Lábrea. This one church, farther upriver, had been started by the Dutch mission and had been active for about ten years. A church building still stood but was no longer active because the pastor had moved to town.

"As far as I know, this was the only church in a rural village of the municipality since Lábrea was founded in 1871," he explained.

We arrived in Samauma in late afternoon. Senhor Pedro and his two youngest sons met us as we descended the gangplank of the river trader's boat. Approaching Senhor Pedro's house, Afonso pointed out six white crosses against the fence near the veranda. Since his hands were full he pointed with his lips, puckering them in that direction. I had learned this was a common way of pointing in Brazil, as you always seem to have your hands full.

"They had fourteen children, but six died before the age of two," Afonso whispered to us.

Just then Pedro's wife, Isabel, appeared in the doorway. She welcomed us with a big smile, then yelled at the two boys who had begun hitting each other after putting our bags down. Then, like she had a split personality, she turned back to us with a big smile and indulged us with flattery.

She unlocked a room for us to hang our hammocks in, then she went to the kitchen to get us a drink. The long narrow storage room had a queasy mixture of smells and was filled with supplies like oil, gasoline, and foodstuffs that Senhor Pedro would trade to community residents at inflated prices. It also contained things he received in exchange—cassava, latex rubber, cacao pods, Brazil nut husks the size of large grapefruits, and monster-sized salted catfish fillets the size of my torso.

Isabel had drinks on a faux silver tray waiting for us outside on the veranda. By the color, I assumed it was pineapple juice. But it was clear, with no fruit pulp to indicate it was juice. Afonso must have seen me studying the drinks.

"It's been a number of months," he said as he lifted his glass. Then in a Hail Mary prayer he said, "Blessed are you—water of the Puru," and gulped it down.

Surmising that such water had caused the death of the six children, I declined a drink, telling Isabel I'd just had one on the boat. Josephine glared at me. She would never tell a lie, even if it meant the death penalty. She took a glass with a smile, then asked Isabel to show us around the house. As Isabel turned inside, Josephine emptied her glass onto the ground.

Senhor Pedro and Isabel's house was the only one in Samauma with a galvanized tin roof. The other ten or twelve houses were thatch-roofed and much smaller. Like other Amazon landowners, they had generated a measure of wealth compared to landless peasants, who required permission to rent and built on land. A landlord living in the community seemed to be the best scenario for Ribeirinhos, as a present landlord sought to create and maintain a good community life, because he was part of it. Senhor Pedro and Isabel were a case in point. Their invitation to us to bring health care would benefit the community, not just them.

The next day we said good-bye to Afonso. He and Senhor Pedro's three oldest sons, Claudio, Adalcír, and João, paddled two small canoes across the Purus and up a small tributary to a trail. From there they helped Afonso carry his gear into the Jarawara village.

We met only a few other families. The communities were small and very isolated, so Josephine and I struggled to think how we would fill our time and keep busy should we move here.

A Catholic friar arrived late in the afternoon. He had previously arranged to stay that night in Samauma. We asked if we could return with him to Lábrea, to which he was agreeable. The next day we said good-bye and joined the friar on a small but tidy riverboat. He yarned on all day about how he came to Lábrea as a missionary from Spain decades ago and described what it was like way back then. He spoke with great pride how his native Spain, Italy, Ireland, and Malta trained and exported priests worldwide. He said the Catholic Church was now exporting Nigerian, Indian, Vietnamese, and Filipino priests as missionaries to the United States and Australia.

I had never thought of missionaries being *exported*, as he put it. We came to Brazil through seeking and hearing God, and raised our own money to get here and stay here. It highlighted to me how different the faith mission model was to what the friar was describing.

TWENTY-FOUR

Not Against Flesh and Blood

BACK home in Manaus we reunited with our girls, Sasha, two and a half, and Chloe, one and a half years old. A few weeks after our visit to Lábrea, while I was playing with the girls in the backyard, Josephine was removing washing from the clothesline. As she did, she noticed she was bleeding from the pregnancy. She urgently called us over to pray. Together, the four of us asked God to stop the miscarriage and protect the life of the little baby in "mummy's tummy." After prayer Josephine went to our bedroom to lie down, and I called the doctor. The doctor told Josephine to remain in bed for a week and advised us against moving, especially to Samauma, as doing so might further jeopardize the pregnancy.

I knew the construction of a boat would take some time, and since I had money in the bank for this purpose, I decided to return to Lábrea alone to get that started. Before I left, however, Josephine developed a high fever. Because she was pregnant, the doctor requested an ultrasound. We were excited to hear the baby's heartbeat for the first time.

The technician said the doctor would need to speak with us, so we waited about ten minutes until he came in.

"The ultrasound has revealed two things," he said while exhaling loudly. "The first thing it shows me is that Josephine is carrying twins."

Our eyes and mouths widened in unison at the news. Then Josephine's face lit up with joy. She'd always dreamed of having twins.

"But wait," the doctor said, pointing sternly at Josephine. "Although one twin appears to be strong and healthy, I am sorry to inform you that the other twin has died."

From elation to devastation in two sentences—we were distraught.

"I'm sorry. But God willing, a healthy child will be born in about six months."

There was no need for a procedure. The twin had died at less than ten weeks and was so tiny that it would be absorbed into the healthy pregnancy. We left, grieving the loss of our little one that we would never know on this earth. But after considering the answer to our prayers—that God stopped a miscarriage and protected the life of one child—we were soon giving thanks for the victorious little one in the womb.

I traveled to the Wycliffe Bible Translators center in Porto Velho, where I met Sandra, the missionary to the Jarawara. From there we flew into Lábrea. In the port, no one knew of any boats going upriver as far as Samauma that day or the next. The delay enabled me to meet with the boatbuilder, who happened to be in town. He said the floodwaters were receding, so if I wanted a boat hull built this year, the trees would need to be floated out of the jungle now. So we signed a contract, and I gave him a $1,500 deposit to get the wood.

On the third day in Lábrea Sandra and I again walked through the port but found no one going upriver. I was feeling sick, so I decided to return to my room at the Dutch mission. Some thirty hours later Sandra came to see how I was. She was surprised to learn I had hardly been out of bed the entire time. After one look at me she said, "I think you should go to the hospital."

"Why do you say that?"

"Look in a mirror," she said.

To my shock, my skin and the whites of my eyes were yellow. The Lábrea hospital diagnosed me with hepatitis and gave me a referral to the Instituto de Medicina Tropical do Amazonas in Manaus, together with a priority pass on the next flight out of town.

The next day in Manaus a specialist at the tropical hospital took my medical history. I told him the hepatitis was diagnosed in Lábrea.

"Ooh, that's not good," he responded.

"Why is that?"

"Haven't you heard of Lábrea Fever?"

"No," I said with fear in my voice.

"It is a complication of hepatitis, and you die within twenty-four hours." After seeing me go pale, he continued, "Don't worry. If you had it, you would be dead already."

I had hepatitis A and was ordered onto a strict diet and bed rest for the rest of the month of May. Local friends gathered leaves from a special plant and made an amazingly effective home remedy, and my speedy recovery astounded the doctor.

However, the accumulated humidity of the seven-month rainy season had turned our lungs into bacterial sponges, resulting in Josephine and me falling sick at the same time with chest infections. For three days we could hardly get out of bed and had to give each other injections. We became so discouraged that we began discussing our options if we left Brazil.

One day, after we were feeling better, Reinaldo and Bráulia came for a visit. We had a nice lunchtime conversation that turned into soul searching. Bráulia, who chooses to avoid small talk, went straight to the point. "How can you justify living in this house in such a beautiful neighborhood, while the JOCUM family is living in army tents on the YWAM property with almost no food to eat? The disparity is grotesque."

Bráulia's turn of phrase often came across as combative. Maybe it was her Marxist upbringing, but in any case, her razor-sharp intellect usually hit the target, and this was no exception.

"You're right, the contrast is extreme. But the Manaus base is an empty piece of land with no running water, electricity, or phone connection," I said.

Reinaldo added bluntly, "No one in YWAM Brazil lives off base."

"Are you suggesting we should live in a tent with two small children?" Josephine asked.

"Mario and Jaçiara are. The directors of YWAM Manaus are living in a tent, while you, as their staff, are living in this nice house," Reinaldo replied.

"Well, they don't have two small children," Josephine stated.

Reinaldo responded without missing a beat, "The founders of YWAM, Loren and Darlene Cunningham, had two small children when they moved into a derelict hotel in Hawaii to pioneer the University of the Nations."

There was a long pause. Last year we had thought our Brazilian coworkers were offended by our decision to learn language for a year, but now we realized that the main point of contention was economics. By using our inheritance to buy a car and a house, we thought we were making a sacrifice by investing all in Brazil. The Brazilians viewed it quite the opposite, however, as avoiding sacrifice.

"Sacrifice is required for all missionaries," Bráulia said. "Neither Jim and Pam Stier, the founders of YWAM Brazil, or Gerson and Elisa, the founders of YWAM Amazon, have sought the comfort of a home off base. They have sacrificed. We have sacrificed. You guys need to show your commitment to the YWAM family and sacrifice too."

"Well, we are not going to sacrifice our children." Josephine said firmly. "Our children's safety is our responsibility, not yours, or anyone else's. We will not be moving to the river's edge, where our children run the risk of drowning."

Josephine looked to me, wanting some backup. *Why aren't you saying anything?* her stare implied.

"Bráulia and Reinaldo," I began slowly, "we genuinely admire the huge sacrifices you have made to live among the Suruwahá."

"And we admire Loren and Darlene, Jim and Pam, and all those who have made sacrifices to build YWAM," Josephine added.

"We also admire the sacrifice of the YWAMers living in tents on the land right now," I said. "But . . . 'to obey is better than sacrifice,' that is what the Bible says. We are living in this house in obedience, because through prayer God directed us to buy it. Sacrifice is important, and equality in the family is important, but living in obedience and in the fear of the Lord, I would have to say, is even more important."

"Point well taken, but maybe it's time to sell this house and be more part of the family," Bráulia said.

Then in a conciliatory tone of voice Reinaldo said, "In all honesty, we are trying to help you. It looks really bad—you guys living in the comfort of this house with the Brazilian YWAMers living in poverty and hardship on the river's edge."

"OK, we can see it now. Thank you for your feedback. We really do appreciate your honesty. We'll pray about whether we should sell this house and move to the YWAM land," I said.

"Great. Prayer is a good way to start," Reinaldo concluded.

"What we have been prayerfully considering is moving to the interior," Josephine said.

"Really? That would be awesome," Bráulia encouraged.

I shared how I had commissioned the construction of a boat hull in Lábrea and told them about our visit to the community of Samauma and our intention to move there.

"I hope you can see that living here is only for a short season and that a nice house or lifestyle is not our goal, or motivation, for moving to the Amazon," Josephine explained.

"We can see that now," Reinaldo acknowledged.

"But I need to remind you that, rightly or wrongly, you have work to do to win back the trust of JOCUM. Don't forget, as family, we are your flesh and blood," Bráulia concluded.

TWENTY-FIVE

A Time to Serve

W E knew we could not move to the interior until after the baby was born. On top of the discouragement we had been battling with, we had no idea what we would do next. Thinking about the rest of the year left us feeling in limbo. Then Reinaldo and Bráulia surprised us with yet another visit. After our last conversation, we were somewhat tentative toward them, but they dispelled our fear with an amazing request.

"We would like you to pray about joining us in Tribal Ministries," Reinaldo said.

"Really?" Josephine and I said in obvious surprise.

"We think your calling to the Ribeirinhos fits better under Tribal Ministries than under YWAM Manaus," Bráulia said. "But until the timing of your move to the interior becomes clear, you could continue to serve here as YWAM Manaus staff. Pray about it."

Reinaldo and Bráulia's invitation communicated such acceptance that our discouragement disappeared and new hope was birthed within us. After some days of prayer, God confirmed we were to join Tribal Ministries and work under Reinaldo and Bráulia as our leaders. As we prayed about what to do for the rest of the year, I felt we were to keep serving in Manaus. Josephine felt more specifically that we were to "do the groundwork." Then I had a thought around the idea of "prepare yourself." It is always good to hear from God. Except in this case, we didn't know what those two phrases meant for us to do.

One day on the YWAM base, in a conversation with Mario about finances, he said he had decided to spend the $6,000 we had in the bank on a truck. I boldly suggested spending only $3,000 on a truck so we could spend $3,000 on bulldozing the property.

"What do we need a bulldozer for?"

"To develop the riverfront property in accordance with the master plan."

He looked at me like I was crazy, clearly not conceptualizing what I was suggesting.

"Look at the property, Mario." I specifically pointed out hundreds of tree stumps. "A bulldozer could remove those with ease. It could make a perimeter road at the back of the property and a gradual sloping road to the water along the far boundary. Then it could make a third internal road to access the buildings."

"It could make a soccer field in the center," Mario said.

"A perfectly level soccer field, Mario, with no stumps. We could have the excess soil pushed to the front of the property and create a new buildable area overlooking the river."

"That would be a great spot to build a house," Mario said.

I could tell that Mario was now seeing my vision.

"Yeah, a bulldozer is a good idea. Why don't you look into it."

"I did already," I said to Mario's surprise. "A bulldozer working nearby will finish at the end of the week."

Instead of agreeing, however, Mario was suddenly backpedaling. "I won't get a very good truck for only $3,000."

"Maybe not," I replied. "But if we do the groundwork with manpower and shovels, it will be three years of hard labor, literally. On the other hand, if we hire the bulldozer, the whole property will be clean, laid out, and ready for development in three days."

Mario conceded that bulldozing was a smart choice, so he asked me to arrange it. Then, after further discussion, he asked me to take the lead on the property development and to look after the *São Mateus.*

"OK, I'll pray about it."

Back home I shared with Josephine my conversation with Mario. She immediately replied, "If you take the lead on property development you will literally 'do the groundwork.'"

"Wow, of course."

"'Do the groundwork' is about serving through developing the Manaus property," Josephine said.

"It makes sense. I'm really excited about it."

"What about 'prepare yourself'? What do you think that means?" Josephine asked.

"Well, by taking responsibility for the *São Mateus,* we can prepare ourselves by starting to minister to River People who live near the Manaus base."

Although we knew God had spoken earlier, we didn't really understand what it meant until these circumstances lined up around us.

Over the next week the bulldozer did an amazing job and Mario bought a "not so good" truck. With the responsibilities for the property development and the *São Mateus,* my motivation increased dramatically, as did my prayer life. One day I got the idea of asking builders, through our newsletter, to leave the cold Minnesota winter to come help build the YWAM base. Josephine thought that was a good idea, but after prayer, she felt we should go to America to recruit and to believe God for six teams. Mario and Jaçiara got really excited about her idea. It seemed audacious, yet something we might be able to achieve.

After church on September 24 we went to a nice hotel for lunch. The hotel had a large pool that Sasha and Chloe loved to swim in. By midafternoon, however, Josephine was having labor pains, so we cut short our pool time and headed to the hospital. Sometime after midnight a strong, vibrant baby girl was born. The Brazilian nurses called her "little tomato" because her skin was cherry red and she beamed with vitality. We named her Alexandra Victoria, because of her victorious survival in the womb.

Only one week after Alexandra's birth, Mario and I flew to São

Paulo. A Korean church had decided to donate a VW van to YWAM Manaus. This was a marvelous provision, considering Mario's sacrifice in buying a "not so good" truck. Together with two Korean pastors, we drove to Brasília, where I would get Alexandra's passport and Josephine's US visa for our recruiting trip. We picked up Jaçiara, who had just flown in from Manaus, as she and Mario had an interview at the US Embassy. After their interview we stayed in a backpackers hostel for the night, waiting and praying. The next day, as an American citizen, I could enter the embassy much faster than everybody else, so I retrieved the passports and returned to the van.

"I got a visa," Mario declared.

"I got one too!" Jaçiara shouted with glee.

We were afraid the embassy would deny Jaçiara, so this was great news. Both were granted a six-month visa, enabling them to stay on to study English after our recruitment tour. As I was looking at Alexandra's cute one-week-old baby photo in her passport, the VW van revved to life and pulled away from the embassy. Then I opened Josephine's passport. Stamped in red across the returned application form: DENIED.

"Josephine has been denied," I yelled.

"What?" Mario and Jaçiara exclaimed in unison.

"Turn around," I yelled in Portuguese, and then in English to the Korean pastor driving the van. But he did not understand.

Mario, Jaçiara, and I gesticulated wildly until the Korean pastor understood.

I marched back into the embassy. "I am an American citizen. How can you deny my wife the right to visit her family in America?"

"Your wife has been out of America for more than two years, so her green card expired. Therefore, she has to reapply for US residency," the consular agent explained.

"That takes months, costs thousands of dollars, and makes no sense. We no longer reside in the United States, nor do we plan to. We are going to show off our new baby to the grandparents."

"I'm just telling you the policy. Here is the form for a US residency visa. Your wife will need to fly to Rio for an interview, get medical checks—"

"Keep the form. I would like to speak to your manager."

"My manager is the US consul, and he will only speak to people appealing his decision. So fill out another form and write 'appeal' on top."

So I filled out another tourist visa application and handed it back.

"Where is the additional supporting evidence? No sense lodging an appeal with the same information you submitted previously."

"Good point. Thanks for the tip. Give me your fax number and I will have supporting information faxed to you overnight."

That evening John Tanner and Parkside Baptist Church faxed supporting letters from Australia, and my parents and my pastor from Redeemer Lutheran Church in Minnesota did the same. Back in Manaus Josephine found our car title, our home title, and the explanatory papers she had received with her green card and faxed them to the consulate as well.

The next day I met the US consul. He was a short, slightly overweight, middle-aged American who looked like the local barber I went to as a kid. We sat in a small room just off the waiting area of the visa section. He plopped my file down on the small table that had my appeal application lying on top. He ceremoniously opened a small box that contained two rectangular rubber stamps, one with a green handle and one with a red handle.

"I received letters of support from Australia and the USA. Your pastor in Minnesota described you as the apostle Paul of the Amazon."

"Maybe you should toss that reference. That's definitely evangel-lastic."

"Ha! Evangel-lastic!" the consul repeated as he let out a deep belly laugh. "Oh man, I haven't heard that one before, and I thought I'd heard it all."

When he finished laughing he said, "Unfortunately, the US government policy is 'once a green card—always a green card.'"

"Can I ask, have you read the green card explanatory papers that my wife faxed through?"

"Oh, I've seen those a hundred times."

"Excuse me, but can I point out that there is not one statement of US government policy, nor is there a statement about retaining US residency in perpetuity in order to have the right to visit the USA. In fact, the section about surrendering your green card if you no longer legally reside in the USA actually communicates the opposite of the government policy."

"I didn't realize that," the consul said while reviewing the explanatory papers.

"The documentation we have provided shows unequivocally that we reside in Brazil. We also have purchased return tickets back to Brazil. Please make an exception to this policy on our behalf. I know you have the power to do so as the US consul."

"You know," the consul said, "I know YWAM. I was the US consul in Athens, Greece, when Don Stephens and Alan Williams of Mercy Ships were charged and prosecuted by the Greek government for proselytizing. The US Embassy supported them in their legal battle."

"That's so cool. One of the Mercy Ships fleet has been to the Amazon twice in two years."

"I'm glad to hear that. I really admired Don and Alan for putting their freedom on the line to change an unjust law. I see that same fight for justice in you. However, I do not have the authority to change US government policy."

My hope faded with those words.

"But, like you said, I do have the power to make an exception."

With that he grabbed the green-handled stamp and stamped APPROVED.

A few weeks later we made our trip to the United States. With our colorful master plan and a daring challenge, we secured eight teams, not six. Because Mario and Jaçiara stayed in the United States to learn English, we were made responsible for receiving and hosting the eight teams and overseeing the development of the YWAM property for the year.

The first team was two couples who surveyed the property, then sited and staked out the location of the future buildings. The second group had a high-tension linesman on their team, so they brought the electricity from the main road and around the entire property. The third and fourth teams built male and female bathrooms and a septic system. They also poured a concrete water tower for the well we had drilled. By April the base had electricity, running water, and sanitation.

During this period, the owner of the property next door offered YWAM the use of his log cabin, in exchange for keeping his property mowed. We had started to build a simple house on the base, out of our own funds, so that we could sell our house in town. But construction was going very slowly. It was only one large room, yet it was already being used as the DTS classroom. Although the log cabin was so severely eaten by termites that the back wall facing the jungle had gaping holes, I saw potential in it for us as a family. Considering our home had served its purpose in helping us get established and learn the language, we felt it was time to put our house up for sale. It sold immediately, even at the ridiculously high price we put on it. We recouped the money we had spent on it, plus all the money we had lost from our inheritance during the global financial crisis.

In the month of May we moved from our family home in town into the log cabin adjacent to the YWAM property. We propped up the main beams to ensure the whole cabin would not fall in on us, and we covered the two gaping holes in the back wall with large wooden wardrobes. The first night before we went to sleep, I saw a large black scorpion scurry out of a termite-eaten hole. I decided to inspect every one of those holes with a hammer and wood chisel. The result was that I killed six large black scorpions in one hour while Josephine read books to Sasha, Chloe, and Alexandra. To keep scorpions out of our beds, we moved them into the middle of the rooms and firmly secured mosquito nets under the mattresses.

With the profit from the sale of our house, I bought a used Toyota Land Rover. The truck would serve the Manaus base now, but later we'd use it for our work in Lábrea. It would enable us to come and go from Lábrea by road, for at least five months of the year, as the town was connected to Porto Velho by the last segment of the Transamazon Highway. I also decided to buy a speedboat from a missionary returning home. I would take family and friends on boat and waterskiing trips occasionally in front of the YWAM base, but it, too, was for our future work in the interior. I bought it should anyone get seriously ill or injured while so far from a town with a hospital.

In nine months the groundwork for developing the riverfront property according to the master plan was done: hundreds of stumps were removed; the roads were graded; there was electricity, a well, a water tower with water to all buildings; and one large dormitory was completed and the foundation for a second was prepared. Various temporary buildings were built on a row of terraced building platforms. The school for the Ribeirinho children was full and operating, there was a perfectly level soccer field in the center of the property, and Mario and Jaçiara, now back from the United States, began building themselves a house in the new area overlooking the river.

We had fulfilled God's two words about serving: to prepare ourselves and to do the groundwork. We also sensed that it was time for a new season of ministry.

PART FIVE

Feeling the Heat

For though we live in the world,
we do not wage war as the world does.

2 CORINTHIANS 10:3

TWENTY-SIX

A Boat and a Jungle House

THE Lord was stretching YWAM Amazon ministries through expansion and effectiveness in ministry. Reinaldo and Bráulia were leading not only the Tribal Ministries but also the new YWAM property in Porto Velho and its training schools. When newlyweds Márcia and Suzuki returned to Porto Velho, they were asked by Reinaldo and Bráulia to assume responsibility for their work in the Suruwahá and for the boat they had renamed the *Abí*. During a weekend in September with the Porto Velho Tribal Ministries leadership team, I got to know Suzuki and Márcia much better. In one of our conversations, they said they did not want to go to and from the Suruwahá by boat because the time and cost was greater than chartering the Wycliffe Bible Translators airplane. From Porto Velho they could fly in and out of the Dení Indian village, then go by canoe down the Cunhuá River and up the Coxodoá, the stream in Suruwahá territory. Even in the dry season a canoe with a regional-style long-tail outboard—basically a lawn mower engine with a propeller on the end of a long shaft—could get them to a point about halfway along the trail to the Suruwahá.

Their plan was to build a house on the banks of the Coxodoá, halfway along the trail. They explained how a house would enable them to come and go from the Suruwahá village more easily and regularly, and how regular retreats to their own jungle house, away from the intensity and inefficiency of the maloca, would advance their linguistic work.

"So how do you propose to get the materials for building a house to the site?" I asked.

"We don't know yet," said Suzuki. "We're thinking a DTS outreach team could help us."

None of my Minnesota friends had come to help build the Manaus base, so I put out another invitation through our newsletter to come to the Amazon to help build a jungle house for Suzuki and Márcia. Almost immediately Jon and Denise Lundberg, a young couple from my church, responded to my request. They could come January through April, which was only three months away. Immediately I shared this news with Suzuki and Márcia and Reinaldo and Bráulia.

Josephine and I talked and prayed about building the jungle house. Ironically, after four years of waiting to do church planting among the River People, I suddenly felt everything was moving too fast, as it meant leaving in just a few months. The boat hull in Lábrea was not started yet. Here in Manaus we were leading the Discipleship Training School, in addition to the daily demands of living in a simple log cabin with three children under four. Life was as busy and demanding as we could take.

Then Márcia phoned. "Oi Kaio, we have some exciting news," she said.

"What's that?"

"Daniel, Fátima, and a team of three guys searching for the Arimadi tribe have agreed to help us build in February and March. If you and Josephine and your builder friend and his wife could come, we would have a team of eleven."

"Don't forget my three girls . . ."

"A team of fourteen, even better!"

"Fourteen people will not fit on the *Abí*, so you should probably ask Mario if you can take the *São Mateus*," I suggested.

"Oh, speaking of the *Abí*," Márcia added, "Suzuki and I spoke with Reinaldo and Bráulia, and they decided to give it to you."

"Give us what?"

"The boat—the *Abí*. With a jungle house, we will not need it for transportation. With Tribal Ministries now based in Porto Velho, Reinaldo said the *Abí* would be better utilized by you and Josephine in Lábrea, instead of being docked so far away in Manaus."

My mind whirled with implications. "That's a game changer."

"That's a what?" Márcia asked, puzzled by the English expression.

"Oh . . . I mean, that's a huge gift. That boat cost $6,000!"

"Actually it cost $7,500," Márcia clarified. "Mercy Ships donated $6,000, and Reinaldo and Bráulia put in $1,500 of their own money."

I was humbled and convicted. In my heart, I had been critical of Reinaldo regarding money, yet he was giving me the *Abí* instead of selling it to me, even though he knew I had money in the bank. The $6,000 I'd reluctantly parted with to buy four boats and motors was returned to me in an instant. It's true: you cannot outgive God.

"Márcia, that's fantastic. Please tell Reinaldo and Bráulia thank you very much."

"I will."

"And thank you too, Márcia."

"You're welcome, Kaio."

"This instantly confirms something."

"What's that?" Márcia asked.

"That we should help you build your jungle house!"

"Oh, that's wonderful," Márcia said.

After I hung up the phone, my thoughts flashed back to the trail, the hike, the maloca, and the Suruwahá people. I never thought I would return there in a million years, let alone return with my family on our own riverboat.

Reinaldo and Bráulia also called us, and encouraged us even further by inviting us to base ourselves with them in Porto Velho. We agreed with their wisdom, as it was much closer to Lábrea than Manaus was. Through a Christian friend we were able to get our belongings, even our truck, on a commercial barge for free, but it was departing in a few days. The Madeira River near Porto Velho sometimes gets too low for large commercial navigation between mid-October and Christmas, so this would be the last trip until next year.

In a mad flurry, we sorted and packed what was for Porto Velho and what was to be left behind in Manaus. Then a couple of truck trips got everything onto the barge just in time. Bags of cement were piled high, like small mountains on top of two barges, which were lashed together and pushed by a super powerful triple-deck tugboat. The hold spaces were empty, leaving plenty of room to store our furniture and personal belongings. Our freezer, refrigerator, and truck couldn't fit underneath, but they just fit in the narrow space between the cement and the front edge of the barge.

Back on the YWAM Manaus base, while I was leading the DTS, two guys looked after the *São Mateus* and the *Abi* riverboats for me. This involved pumping water out of the wooden hulls as needed and pushing them out to deeper water as the water receded. During the dry season, the Amazon can recede many feet down the bank in just one day. At Manaus there's a fifty-foot vertical difference between high-water and low-water season, but being hundreds of feet deep, the Amazon never gets too shallow for navigation.

One afternoon the two guys were not able to push the *Abi* off the bottom. As they had left this job until evening, everyone who could help was cleaned up and eating dinner, so they decided to wait until morning to get help from others. The next morning, however, the *Abi* was so beached that all the men on the base could not push it free. I went on board the *São Mateus* to use it to pull the *Abi* free, but the battery was dead, so I put on the battery charger and returned to class. By late afternoon, however, it was too late; the *Abi* had tipped forty-five degrees onto its side. I drove to the builder I had contracted to construct new sleeping quarters on the *Abi*. He advised me to dig a channel, buy a hundred feet of rope as thick as my wrist, and to dig a six-foot-deep hole into the riverbank.

The boatbuilder arrived early the next morning. While students and staff dug a channel in the bank deep enough to refloat the *Abi*, the boatbuilder wrapped the hundred-foot rope around the hull and back up the bank. Then he bolted four beams together in an X shape to a pre-cut tree trunk we had dropped into the six-foot-deep hole. This enabled eight men to push all together against the beams, two per beam. The giant tree-trunk cog turned like a winch. For the entire day we worked like the slaves of Egypt, manually lifting incredible weight through simple tools of leverage. The *Abí* raised inch by inch until it was upright and slid into the channel. We tied the *São Mateus* to the back of the *Abí* and pulled it backward off the beach until it floated freely once again. It was a colossal effort.

TWENTY-SEVEN

More Than a Mishap

ONE week after raising the *Abi* there was a message from Porto Velho: "Your truck has been totaled out. Call urgently." My friend Dave Irving had volunteered to get our stuff off the barge and store it at the Porto Velho base for me. I immediately thought he'd had a serious accident driving back to the YWAM base in my truck, but when I called, it was Dave who answered.

"Sorry to be the bearer of bad news, but your truck is toast."

"Did it catch on fire?" I asked.

"Not toast like 'burnt'—toast like 'totally smashed.'"

"How in the world did it get smashed on top of a barge?"

"The barge captain said he went over a large tree floating in the river," Dave explained. "He said floating trees get pushed off to the side or underneath by the force and weight of the barge. But due to exceedingly low water, the roots of the tree were rammed into a sandbar. As the barge moved forward, the top of the tree and a series of heavy branches then hit the side of your truck, totally smashing the cab, the truck bed, and the fiberglass topper."

"I don't believe it."

"The captain couldn't believe it either," Dave continued. "If you hadn't chained your truck to the barge, he said it would have been catapulted into the river."

I flew to Porto Velho the next morning. Sadly, everything Dave said was true. Yet surprisingly, the truck was drivable, as the engine and drivetrain were not affected. I unloaded our belongings off the barge and stored them at the Porto Velho base. After inquiring with my friend who had arranged the barge, I learned that my truck was not covered by their insurance because it was not on their manifest as commercial cargo. Since I had no collision insurance, the repair bill was all mine and would certainly be thousands of dollars.

Back in Manaus, the DTS lecture phase finished and the students went on outreach. I hired a welder to build a metal stairway up the back of the *Abi*, and the local boatbuilder constructed our family sleeping quarters on the roof. In early December we moved out of the log cabin in Manaus and flew to Porto Velho to set up our accommodation on the base there.

An Australian couple who had responded to our invitation to volunteer in the Amazon was already serving at YWAM Porto Velho. Keith was a mechanic. But more than that, he was able to fix just about anything. After looking at the smashed truck, he gave me a small list of tools he needed and immediately went to work on it. Keith repaired everything. The only thing I paid for was the repainting that a local professional did. On Christmas Eve it was done.

The day after Christmas we embarked on a three-thousand-mile family trip from Porto Velho south to Brasília in central Brazil, then back up northeast to the annual staff meeting in Belém. Halfway there, while in Brasília, our truck was broken into while in a shopping center parking lot. Alexandra's portable crib and our garment bag, filled with our dress clothes, were pulled out of the truck topper through a small side window. Lucky for us, the suitcases didn't fit through. This was the third depressing mishap in as many months.

After the YWAM Amazon staff meeting, Reinaldo and Bráulia

drove our truck the three thousand miles back to Porto Velho. We, on the other hand, returned to Manaus to finish preparations on our riverboat home. We stayed at Don and Teresa's, who had built a few rooms of their house on the Manaus base before they went on furlough for a number of months. Jon and Denise Lundberg also arrived, as did Dale Olson. All three were friends from Redeemer who came to help me modify the *Abí*.

One Sunday after church we went out to lunch in a truck our pastor in Manaus had loaned to us. Because of a midafternoon tropical downpour, Jon, Denise, and Dale returned by bus instead of riding in the bed of the truck. Arriving back at Don and Teresa's house on the base, Josephine waited with the kids in the truck until I got the door open. After a dash through the rain I was shocked to see that the door was already open. Worse yet, the lock and door handle were broken off with an axe. The axe was still there, leaning against the doorframe.

"Wait there," I yelled through the rain, "I think we've been broken into."

I picked up the axe and pushed the door open slowly. My heart pounded faster at the thought of an intruder. I poked my head inside and saw light and rain coursing through a large hole in the roof over the bedroom. I wandered back and flung the door open. It was a charred smoking mess, open to the watery heavens—our room was gutted by fire. The children's room was spared, but Josephine and I lost everything in our suitcases.

Moving out of Don and Teresa's house and back into the derelict log cabin on the neighbor's property was disheartening. For the rest of January Denise, Josephine, and I cleaned smoke off every wall in the house while Jon and Dale rebuilt the bed frame, storage shelves, and the temporary kitchenette Don and Teresa had in their bedroom. We replaced roof sheeting, the mattress, the door, the bedroom window, and the electrical switches that were destroyed by the fire. Josephine and I surmised that in our rush out the door for church we forgot to unplug the electric element we had used for heating water. The kettle must have boiled dry and caught the tablecloth on fire, which in turn ignited the bed. YWAMers saw smoke billowing from the house and broke into it with an axe to put out the flames.

By the first of February, the day we had originally planned to leave, the local boatbuilder finished the sleeping quarters on the *Abi*. Barring any other strange and destructive mishaps, I calculated the *Abi* would be ready for our maiden voyage in a month.

TWENTY-EIGHT

The *Abí*

OUR inherited riverboat gift was originally built for a retired university professor who used it like a motor home, relaxing and writing books while floating through the wilds of the Amazon. He named it *Chaluh*, after his niece, who some years later received it as an inheritance. She sold it to Reinaldo and Bráulia, who renamed it *Abí*—a Suruwahá word that means both "fire" and "father." Both of those Suruwahá words are associated with the source of life.

The *Abí* was a regional-style riverboat, which means that the deep V-shaped wooden hull flattens out underneath by midship. This design results in only a three-foot draw, enabling a relatively large boat to navigate shallow water.

The captain's wheelhouse sits on top of a triangular foredeck, where the mooring ropes and the gangplank are kept. Behind the wheelhouse is a main room, twelve by nine feet in size, with a built-in sofa on one side and a table and chairs on the other. A large cupboard sits at the end of the room. An insulated engine housing, creating an engine room, covers a truck-sized diesel engine, mounted exactly in the middle at the bottom of the hull. On the right side is a bathroom and on the left is the galley. The galley door goes onto the aft deck that has a countertop with a laundry sink on one side and a tiny cabin on the other.

My plan for living long-term among the Ribeirinhos was to transform the *Abí* into a riverboat home. The key to this transformation was private sleeping quarters on the roof. This would allow the main floor to be used for daily living and public interaction. To do this the boatbuilder attached beams on each side of the engine housing up through the ceiling to create a five-by-twelve-foot sleeping quarters with several windows for good ventilation. Safe access to this room was via a full stairway at the back, built on heavy steel beams protruding from the rounded stern.

The new sleeping quarters was fitted with a double-bed mattress and three hammocks for the girls suspended over our feet. The stairway, the back of the boat, and the entire rooftop was fenced in, and we cut the doors in half so they could be fixed at the bottom while opening at the top. Josephine and I wanted absolute certainty that our children could not fall overboard.

Dale Olson and Jon and Denise Lundberg completed the remaining modifications over the next six weeks. Jon and Dale cut a trapdoor to access the space under the main room floor where we put knee-high metal barrels full of supplies and dry food storage sufficient for three months. Between this space and the engine was a three-hundred-gallon fuel tank. At eight miles to the gallon the *Abí* could travel 2,400 miles between fill-ups. However, we needed a lot of gasoline for the portable generator and for fueling the speedboat's big outboard. Jon and Dale devised enough space to fit three fifty-five-gallon metal fuel drums by cutting a hole in the floor under the built-in sofa. It was perfect. One drum I filled with diesel for the generator, and I filled the other two drums with gasoline. We cut portholes next to them to prevent gasoline fumes from building up under the floor and blowing us sky-high.

I decided to run the *Abí*'s diesel generator from six to ten o'clock each evening, which was long enough to have lights for dinner and evening activities and would allow us to run fans to assist in getting us to sleep in the suffocating Amazon heat and humidity. However, four hours of electricity is not enough to keep a fridge or a freezer cold, so having those wasn't an option.

We were six weeks behind schedule, but everything was finally done. The modifications worked well to create both a riverboat home and a ministry vessel. Suzuki and Márcia and the Arimadi team had been waiting about a month in Manaus. They had asked Dave and Elizabeth, who had begun church planting upriver in a Ribeirinho community, if they would travel with us to help carry cargo and the people who had promised to help build Suzuki and Márcia's jungle home near the Suruwahá. The Ribeirinho community they worked in was only two days from the Suruwahá trailhead—close by Amazon standards.

Over the next week four missionary teams represented by fourteen adults and four children went on a shopping spree, buying everything we might need for the rest of the year. Finally, a huge load of wood for the jungle house—wall studs, floorboards, and wallboards—was delivered. Most was loaded onto the main deck of Dave and Elizabeth's larger boat, but a large pile of short planks covered our main room floor. Both boats were fully laden and sat low in the water.

Four years and four months after moving to Manaus, it was now time to leave. It was sad saying good-bye to our friends at church, especially Cleide, Leonardo, and their families in our old neighborhood. We gave big hugs to Mario and Jaçiara and our many friends on the YWAM base. The partnership to pioneer YWAM Manaus had seemed long and challenging at times, but in hindsight we were amazed at how much was achieved in such a short time.

Last but not least, we said good-bye to Dale Olson. His new love interest, Suzie, was staying on the Manaus base, so he suddenly had no interest in coming with us to build the jungle house. In spite of the many sad good-byes, we were also full of anticipation for the new season before us.

We slept our first night as a family in our sleeping quarters on the roof. The three guys on the Arimadi team, Ezekiel, Nivaldo, and Roberto, slept in hammocks in the main room, while Jon and Denise had the tiny cabin at the back. Dave and I woke up at three in the morning to get our journey off to an early start, but our battery was dead. A piece of insulation had lodged under the float-switch of our automatic bilge pump, which caused it to run all night, depleting the battery. I had a backup battery, so after a quick switch, I started the engine and we left without delay.

It was exciting to be on our way. Our goal was to get to Manacapuru on the northern bank of the Amazon before dark. Dave had an electrician friend there who offered to do a few jobs on both boats while we were in town. After that, we would travel nonstop for about ten days and nights until we arrived at the trailhead to the Suruwahá. The first day went smoothly even though the current was exceedingly strong and fast. We arrived at the Manacapuru wharf around four that afternoon. I moored the *Abí* against the main dock, facing straight into the current, while Dave and Elizabeth tied on the other side of the *Abí* out in deeper water.

Before we walked off into town, we stood on the foredeck of the *Abí* and Jon and Denise took our picture. It was Sunday, March 24, our first day on the boat. We would put that picture in our next newsletter with the caption *The Riverboat Family*—Kent, Josephine, Sasha (four and a half), Chloe (three and a half), and Alexandra (one and a half).

Since this humble town was going to be our last taste of relatively modern civilization for at least two months, I took my girls out to dinner. Then, remembering we would not eat or drink anything cold in the coming months, I bought everyone ice cream.

Before calling it a night, I checked the engine room. Because the automatic bilge pump was wired to the battery that had gone dead, I used the manual pump to extract what little bit of water there was in the hull, then I went to bed. We slept deeply and peacefully until Jon Lundberg's pounding on the door jolted us awake.

TWENTY-NINE

Down but Not Out

"KENT, you better get downstairs quick," Jon's voice boomed.

I opened my eyes and jumped to my feet, all in the same motion. I could feel the equilibrium of the boat was off.

"What is it, Jon?" I prodded as we leapt down the stairs.

"Water is coming into the boat under the floor in our room. The sound woke me up."

Jon and Denise were sleeping in the small back cabin, which originally had a tiny sink with a drainpipe that emptied into the river. I had taken out that sink and cut off the drainpipe. I knew exactly where it was. Even though the drainpipe was below the floor, it was still a good eighteen inches above the water line. If water was coming into that pipe, it meant the hull was seriously low in the water. I went straight to the engine room and threw the doors open.

"Oh my God," we said in unison. The hull was full of water.

"Jon, get Denise and my family off the boat now," I ordered.

"Ezekiel, Nivaldo, Roberto get up! The boat is sinking!" I shouted. "Get your hammocks and your stuff onto Dave and Elizabeth's boat, then get back here and start bailing water." All three were instantly propelled into action.

I leapt onto the wharf to assess the situation but saw no obvious breach of the hull. I did see, however, that the boat was at a critical stage, with the portholes only an inch above the river. If the water reached the portholes, the boat would go down in seconds.

I could see anxious apprehension on Jon's and Josephine's faces as they passed our children to safety onto the second deck of Dave and Elizabeth's boat.

Dave yelled out, asking what he could do. I told him to tie his boat to the *Abí* in as many places as he could.

"But if she goes down, she'll take us with her," Dave hollered back.

"No it won't, Dave!"

I had no confidence that what I said was true, but it did make me realize that the boat needed to be secured on all sides, not just one.

Ezekiel and Nivaldo began bucketing out water as Suzuki and Márcia arrived from the other boat. I asked them to get the wood for their house off the *Abí* to reduce the weight. People started gathering on the wharf because of the commotion, so Suzuki and Márcia began passing planks to total strangers. Jon came back, and I sent him to secure the *Abí* to the wharf. Then I got Roberto to tie up to a neighbor's boat at the front and to yet another boat at the back.

Now that we were bailing water and the boat was being secured, someone had to stop water from pouring in. That someone was me. This meant swimming under the floor to the back of the hull behind the engine room to stuff a rag into the gushing drainpipe. I was aware that if the river reached the portholes while I was under the floor behind the engine, I would not be able to get out. I was the captain, and if anyone has to go down with the ship, it's the captain.

That sounds noble, but I had always imagined drowning to be the worst way to die. If the boat sank while I was under the floor, I couldn't just give up and passively drown. I would fight against the water rushing into the boat to pull myself from under the floor. But the boat would go down fast—ten, twenty, thirty feet in seconds. It would get black and cold, just like death itself. The worst thing would be having time to know I was doomed. If nothing was blocking the engine doors, I would swim out, but then everything would be in the way. The knee-high barrels of supplies and the three fifty-five-gallon drums of fuel would by then be floating on the ceiling of the main room, slowing my escape. Forty to fifty feet down, the boat would hit the bottom of the Amazon River. The pressure would be immense. My lungs would be searing, burning for air, as I continued holding my breath. I would feel anger and anguish at dying young. Not being able to hug my wife and children and say "I love you" would be my dying regret.

I ran back inside the boat and squeezed through the small doors of the engine room and past the guys bailing water. I yelled, "If the *Abí* goes down while I am under the floor, as your captain, I am ordering you to get yourselves out."

They paused momentarily to take in the implications of what I had just said. Then Ezekiel yelled, "Faster, Nivaldo. Pass the bucket!"

I contorted my body past the engine, then addressed Ezekiel again, "But please tell my wife and children that I love them."

"God of mercy, help us all," Ezekiel said in reply, then bucketed even faster.

I took a deep breath and submerged myself under the floor. With my foot against the top of the transmission I extended my body and arm to where the drainpipe was. I stuffed the pipe with a rag until it halted the flow of water. Then with my hands on the underside of the floor I pushed my body backward past the engine and burst out of the water under the engine housing.

"I plugged the leak," I said to Ezekiel as I caught my breath.

"We have two buckets going now," he replied.

I saw Suzuki and Roberto bucketing from the other side. I went to help Márcia remove the last planks off of the main room floor just as some helpful neighbors arrived with a power pump. They dropped it inside the boat through the side door that was now open to the wharf. Nivaldo stopped bucketing and placed the hose of the power pump in the hull full of water as Ezekiel tried to start the pump motor. It wouldn't start. The owner of the pump yelled instructions to Ezekiel, but it still didn't start. Ezekiel told the owner to come and start it himself, but he was afraid to get on the boat. Finally the pump owner and another man stood on the edge of the *Abí* and hoisted it onto the wharf so he could start it from there. As the two heavy men stood on the edge of the hull and lifted the pump, the boat dropped a few inches under their weight. I heard water instantly rush into the gaping portholes.

"Get off the edge of the boat!" I yelled in desperation. But they were too slow. In a matter of seconds the boat began tipping into the wharf and sinking from the stern.

"Get off the boat now!" I screamed to everyone. But the two men wresting the pump off the edge of the boat were blocking the immediate side exit.

"This way, this way!" I yelled and pointed Suzuki, Roberto, Nivaldo, and Ezekiel out the right front door from where they could leap onto the wharf. As the boat went down, everything in the kitchen cupboards fell to the floor, with the stove crashing across the kitchen aisle. Everyone was off but me. Suddenly I was running uphill as the boat was going under. I grabbed the frame of the front door with both hands to prevent myself from falling back into the sinking boat. Josephine was screaming my name hysterically from Dave and Elizabeth's boat until she saw me emerge onto the foredeck. Jon's big hand grabbed my forearm and pulled me onto the wharf as the *Abí* disappeared from beneath my trailing foot.

Those on the wharf, and on Dave and Elizabeth's boat, gazed at the destruction between us, hopelessness and distress on every face. My three sweet babies had tears rolling down their cheeks in perfect empathy with the distraught faces of Elizabeth, Denise, and Josephine, who held them. I looked at my watch. I don't know why. I guess that's what you do when someone, or something, dies. It was 6:55 a.m.

Then something surprising happened. The big heavy ropes, as thick as my wrist, held the *Abí*. Hope emerged in every gazing eye as the roof of our sleeping quarters remained above the murky darkness and stood firm against the powerful Amazon current. Just then, various items burst to the surface and streamed out the back in the swirling current.

"Get your canoes and catch the stuff!" Suzuki yelled to everyone around.

I stood on the wharf in a daze, watching people frantically paddle around plucking clothes, pillows, bottles, toys, books—anything that floated—from the river. After years of training and intense preparation, this was the result of our first day of ministry as a riverboat family. With that thought, I came to the verge of a total breakdown. The trauma of the past minutes was so palpable in my chest that my only wish was to be transported home to Minnesota so I could crawl into my cool bed in my dark room and hibernate for six months. But I couldn't. I was sitting on a wharf in the heat of the Amazon. I didn't want to be captain right then—but I was—so I tried to hide my despair. More than that, I was a husband and a father—so I had to continue. I was also a missionary—I had put my hand to the plow, and there was no turning back.

The *Abi* was three-quarters of the way down, but holding fast. If it had gone to the bottom, there would have been no hope. But now there was hope, although I had no idea what to do.

The man with the power pump leaned down and said to me that he would advise the local boatyard for me.

"Thank you very much," I said. But I couldn't look him in the eye. We were winning the battle until he and his friend had stood on the edge. I think he knew that too. Maybe he was showing penance by offering to help. Then again, I couldn't hold him responsible for the *Abi* sinking. Before he showed up we were already an inch from disaster.

Then I thought, "Praise God Jon woke up." If he hadn't woken, the ten of us on board would have gone down to a watery grave. The thought of that made me shudder.

Two hours later, a huge boat from the boatyard arrived. Suzuki, Dave, and I boarded and spoke with the man in charge.

"Two boats, maybe three, have gone down here," he said. "But this is the first one to be recovered. You gringos have such dumb luck."

"It's not luck. It's God's protection," Suzuki said boldly.

"Well, if it's not luck, then I say it's the money. I've never seen such money spent on mooring ropes as heavy duty as those holding your boat."

Dave, Suzuki, and I looked at each other and smiled, knowing the story behind the thick ropes. It was Monday morning, March 25. The *Abi* was towed to the boatyard, and by noon it was getting winched up the dry-dock ramp.

Dave's electrician friend generously gave us an empty rental house to live in. It was a kind gesture, but the house was completely unfurnished, with only intermittent electricity and water. We walked across the street twice a day to get clean drinking water from our neighbor's well and carried it back in buckets.

Everything the ten of us owned—sheets, pillows, hammocks, towels, and every item of clothing was stained by the dirty water, boat oil, and diesel fuel. We had to walk three blocks to the home of a Christian family who let us use their washing machine. It was so old I hadn't seen anything like it since I was a little kid at my grandmother's house. It had no spin cycle, so when a load was done, we carried the heavy wet washing three blocks back to the house to dry. Since it was the humid rainy season, dry it did not. When the electricity was on, we ironed everything to dry it before it got moldy.

Late one afternoon Jon and Denise took the three girls out to play. Josephine took the opportunity to walk into a vacant lot near the house. I saw her put down her cup of tea and cry out to God. She is a high achiever, so waiting around with nothing to do was challenging. But then I heard prayers of desperation much deeper than impatience. I knew she felt as devastated by the sinking as I did. We were finding it hard to be strong for each other; we were both severely weakened by the trauma. It was an agonizing test.

Our children helped by bringing joyful normalcy to each day. They appeared unfazed by the tumultuous circumstances and happily played with Jon and Denise and children in the neighborhood while Josephine and I attended to a multitude of tasks.

On the third day after the boat sank, everyone gathered on Dave and Elizabeth's boat to resolve what to do. The *Abí* hull was being recaulked and was progressing well. However, work on the engine and generator had yet to commence, so I had no firm idea when we could resume our journey.

After group prayer two things were agreed on. The first was "time is of the essence." Jon and Denise had to fly out of the Dení Indian village on May 13, only six weeks away, yet arrival was still a minimum of ten days away. The second area of agreement was "it is war." Most of the team confessed they'd been complacent in spiritual warfare. Of course there would be tremendous demonic opposition to the gospel being preached to an unreached people group. Stopping an army's arrival is a fundamental tactic of war. Everyone felt that God's solution was to stay the course, get upriver as fast as possible, and build the house while fighting the spiritual battle. Someone said that God had brought the story of Nehemiah to mind, which confirmed the idea of building and doing battle at the same time.

Dave and Elizabeth offered to take everyone to the Coxodoá stream, where everything could be shuttled to the building site by canoe with a long-tailed outboard. So we renewed our commitment to build the jungle house, with or without the *Abí*. Everyone would go except my family and Ezekiel and Nivaldo, who would stay behind to help me navigate the boat. If we got to the Suruwahá in time to help, great. If not, well, the jungle house would be built without us.

On Easter Sunday, March 31, we waved good-bye to Jon and Denise, Márcia and Suzuki, and everyone else on Dave and Elizabeth's boat.

THIRTY

The Maiden Voyage

T W O days later the *Abí* reentered the water. Zezinho confirmed that he would help us travel upriver. He had more experience navigating than Ezekiel, Nivaldo, and I put together, and more importantly, he knew the high-water season shortcuts that could save us two or three days' travel time.

The next day, Ezekiel and Nivaldo shared that they felt the boat was unstable, being too high for its width, and suggested removing the top room I had recently built. They had overheard men repairing the hull say that the boat was unsafe. I acknowledged the *Abí* was top-heavy for the wide and windy Amazon, but its design was not unsafe on tributaries like the Purus River.

On April 7, exactly two weeks after we left Manaus, we resumed our trip. Perfect weather and Zezinho's experience brought us confidence as we crossed from the north bank to the south bank of the Amazon River. By midmorning, however, the wind picked up so that the boat bounced and shuddered with each wave impact. Ezekiel and Nivaldo were clearly fearful. We traveled in rain and pierced two-foot waves for ten hours straight. With a top speed of five miles per hour into the waves and the strong current, we did not cover the seventy miles needed to make it to the Purus River before dark. This created a dilemma. Ezekiel and Nivaldo did not want to sleep on the Amazon for fear of a big storm blowing the top-heavy boat over, but neither did we want to travel in the dark and choppy conditions. Zezinho guided the boat into some willows on the southern bank and shut it down. I was so glad it was Zezinho who announced we needed to stop for the night, because despite their misgivings, Ezekiel and Nivaldo accepted his decision. I doubted they would have accepted it from me.

Early in the morning, I turned the ignition key, and nothing.

"What!" I cried, my stomach suddenly churning. How could the battery be dead? It made no sense. Dave's electrician friend had upgraded the electrical system precisely for this not to happen. The others were waking up, so I decided to calm down over coffee. After breakfast Ezekiel and I attached the second battery in parallel to the first, using the cables the electrician set up for this very purpose.

As Zezinho cranked the engine over and over, the plastic coating on the wires connecting the two batteries overheated and burst into flames.

"Stop, Zezinho! There's fire in the engine room."

Ezekiel grabbed the fire extinguisher, but it was so corroded that he couldn't even pull the pin out to use it. Like all engines, there was grease and diesel fuel everywhere. Some on top of the old battery ignited. Nivaldo grabbed the fire extinguisher from the kitchen but nothing came out. Panic took over as the flames ran up the battery cables to the engine. Ezekiel bolted out of the engine room, and Nivaldo and Zezinho sprinted to the back of the boat to get water from the river. In a frenzy I pounded the flames with my T-shirt. By the time Zezinho and Nivaldo arrived with buckets of water, I had put out the fire. In the six months of refurbishing the boat, I never once thought about the fire extinguishers. It was a bad way to start the day. We started the generator and put the dead battery on the charger while Ezekiel fixed the battery cables. After five hours of charge, the batteries started the engine straightaway. Once again we were on our way, now traveling up the much narrower Purus.

I thought this would bring calm, but for some reason an even greater sense of fear and foreboding seemed to fall upon us.

I was driving the boat with Zezinho when he said that the speedboat should not be chained and padlocked to the back of the boat.

"In the event of an emergency, like the fire this morning, only you can release the speedboat, because only you have the key," he said.

I nodded in agreement. I had kept it locked because of the threat of theft while in port. Now that we were away from the towns, the speedboat could be tied up with ropes so that anyone could untie it in an emergency. I gave Zezinho the key, and he unlocked the speedboat and tied it up with a rope.

After dark, when Josephine went upstairs to get a book for the girls, she noticed that the speedboat was gone. We had no idea if it came loose five hours or five minutes ago. Zezinho was noticeably embarrassed by the news. We immediately turned around and scoured the banks of the river with our spotlights.

This was yet another strange mishap. The sense of foreboding became so thick that everyone felt like it was crushing us. I thought for sure the speedboat was gone forever, but after about an hour of searching, someone spotted it wedged among the willows. It had floated into the trees in such a way that we couldn't quite reach it, even after powering the nose of the *Abí* into the branches. Zezinho, however, was able to clamber along tree branches and reach the boat without entering the water. After retying the speedboat, we restarted the *Abí*, but the engine made such a horrific noise that we shut it off immediately.

"The propeller is caught in branches underwater. Let's use the speedboat to free it."

With the speedboat's powerful engine, we pulled the *Abí* free. Zezinho now had to go into the water to inspect the drive shaft, propeller, and rudder. Thankfully after a few dives, he confirmed there was no damage.

The kids could not concentrate on reading with so much commotion. So once we were on our way again, Josephine called them back to the main room to finish the book. But Alexandra, our one-and-a-half-year-old, was not there. Josephine came to the wheelhouse looking for her.

"I don't have her. She must be in the bedroom."

Josephine fearfully ran through the boat and up the stairs. A moment later, we heard a shriek of desolation that has been engraved on my soul ever since, "Kent, she's not here!"

"That is not possible," I defiantly declared as I stormed into the main room.

Sasha and Chloe looked at me with fear etched on their faces, but I had no time to comfort them. I threw open the engine room doors; it was the only place I could think of where she could possibly fall, but she was not there.

Josephine marched down the stairs yelling bold declarations against the enemy, "You will not take our children!" I raced past her up to our room.

"She has to be here," I said as I ransacked our quarters. "I know I made the boat safe." But she was not there.

Back outside, I scanned the walkways on each side of the bedroom, but she was not there. Anguish was bubbling in my soul like molten lava since Josephine's soul-piercing scream. My mind had kept these emotions capped, refusing to believe Alexandra had fallen into the river. But facts began merging with fear into an eruption of grief that I could no longer contain. Anguish gushed from my soul in violent sobs.

Then I saw her. She was on the elevated deck, in front of our room, standing in between the spotlights with her face pressed into the fencing. She had been too small to get herself up in front of our room, at least until now.

In spite of my indescribable relief, I was unable to fully recap my emotions. Only deep gulps of air brought my sobbing under control. Then I called out loudly for all to hear.

"I found her!"

I tried to disguise the anguish in my voice as I asked, "How did you get up here, sweetheart?"

"Look, Daddy," she said, as her finger followed the spotlight beams scanning the river.

"Yes, pumpkin. Come to Daddy."

As I lifted her into my arms, Josephine arrived absolutely distraught and immediately snatched her from my arms, "Alexandra, my darling."

I hugged them both so tightly that Alexandra began squirming for air. Sasha and Chloe had followed Josephine up the stairs and joined us. I slowly, and gently, walked them all into our bedroom.

Back downstairs, Zezinho was at the helm. Ezekiel and Nivaldo were on either side, each in command of a spotlight.

"Alexandra is safe."

They responded with relieved expressions of "Oh, God be praised" and "Thank you, Jesus."

"I will join Josephine and the kids in the room now," I said. "I can take the helm in the morning. Goodnight."

"Goodnight," they replied in unison.

After we put the girls to bed, Josephine and I cried out to God to deliver us from the spiritual warfare raging against the boat and us in it. We were once again reminded how important this journey was. The Suruwahá were a primitive tribe in danger of extinction because they committed suicide in the belief that they were going to a better place. God had led us to build a jungle house that would help, in a small way, in their journey of deliverance. The enemy, on the other hand, was trying everything in his power to prevent us from accomplishing this goal. But we determined in our hearts that God would have the victory.

THIRTY-ONE

Jungle Shortcuts

I AWOKE around dawn and continued our journey up the Purus. According to the journal Nivaldo had left in the wheelhouse, today was Tuesday, April 9. I had completely lost track of the days. I perused his entries and notations; they read more like a script for a war movie than a travel log. It made me realize that spiritual warfare is not merely a theological concept, nor is it a struggle confined to the heavenly realm; it is also a war played out on earth.

About an hour later Zezinho joined me. He informed me that yesterday's events had left him, Ezekiel, and Nivaldo so depleted that they became too tired to travel through the night, so a little past midnight they stopped to sleep.

"Yesterday was a tough one. But today—by faith—will be better," I said.

"I hope so," Zezinho mumbled unconvincingly.

By late morning Zezinho informed me we were nearing the first jungle shortcut.

"You'd better let me take the wheel as this shortcut can be bad," Zezinho said.

"What do you mean?" I asked.

"The collision of currents creates nasty whirlpools," Zezinho explained. "For a top-heavy boat like the *Abí*, this can cause havoc."

"Are you afraid of the boat too, Zezinho? Keep to the facts," I pleaded. "The boat did not sink because it was top-heavy."

I was surprised by Zezinho's comment. Not having experienced the trauma of the sinking, he had been a pillar of strength to our team. But now he, too, seemed to be plunging into the same irrational fear that Ezekiel and Nivaldo were battling.

We turned off the main channel of the Purus and into the turbulent water of the shortcut. The whirlpools rocked the boat but didn't threaten its stability. But it did create an exaggerated fear in the three guys. What concerned me, however, was what I could see farther ahead—white water. I didn't think anything like rapids could exist on rivers in the flat central basin of the Amazon. But there it was, a quarter-mile in front of us, churning white water cutting straight across our path.

I could instantly calculate that we needed to enter the torrent nose first; otherwise the force of the water against the side of the boat would sweep us downstream and shipwreck us in the trees. Zezinho backed off the engine. There was a small boat directly in front moving slowly.

"Good," I said. "Let him get farther ahead."

I thought it best to give the small boat the space and time it needed to navigate the corner into the fast-moving water, but Zezinho had other ideas. Backing off the engine allowed the current to sweep us downstream to the left of the small boat, and then Zezinho throttled it.

"What are you doing?" I said.

"I'm passing. I'm afraid if we're behind the small boat the current will push her into us."

Ezekiel, Nivaldo, and I could see that we would not pass the small boat in time to get our nose pointing upstream before we entered the fast flow. Zezinho's judgment was way off. I also knew we should be on the right side of the channel. Instead we were on the left, close to the trees, so if the current did sweep us downstream we would have even less time to gain control before we were tangled in the jungle.

"Nivaldo, signal the small boat to back off and move to the right," I ordered.

"Ezekiel, help Josephine get life jackets on the kids, and get us some too."

Many seconds ticked by.

"Am I past the boat?" Zezinho asked agitatedly.

"You can't wait for them. Turn now," I said.

"No, you're not past," Nivaldo replied.

"Turn anyway, Zezinho," I intervened. "They will back off as you turn."

More seconds passed before Zezinho angled right. "Turn now!" I ordered.

Zezinho finally turned hard right, but it was too late. We entered the fast-moving current at a forty-five-degree angle. The force of the engine prevented us from getting swept downstream, but it wasn't sufficient to turn the boat into the force of the current. Like an arm wrestle that fell neither left nor right, the boat kept going straight across the shortcut toward the jungle in front of us. Zezinho's response was to pull harder on the wheel and push harder on the throttle, but that made no difference.

"Get out of the way!" I yelled and pushed Zezinho off the wheel.

I threw back the throttle and gunned it in reverse while spinning the wheel hard left. Working with the current, this threw the rear of the boat left and brought the nose to the right and straight into the current. But this also caused the boat to be swept downstream quickly. Then I threw the wheel right and gunned it. The engine churned heroically, but downstream momentum overpowered us. The speedboat at the back was plunged into the branches of flooded jungle trees before the engine overcame our slide and brought us to a complete standstill. Slowly the boat pushed us forward, away from certain shipwreck, and gained the upper hand in its struggle against the surging current. The victory did not spark spontaneous celebration; rather, we spent the next moments in a trembling recovery. I handed the wheel back to Zezinho and went into the main room.

I found tears rolling down Josephine's fearful face. I wiped them away and helped remove her life jacket as a sign that we were safe. While we removed life jackets from our girls, Josephine looked at me with questioning eyes. I considered asking her if we should turn around. We could literally float downstream to Manaus without expending any effort. We could be done with the battles with a turn of the wheel. That was the easy option. Going upstream is never easy. Fighting the physical and spiritual currents against us meant Ezekiel and Nivaldo finding a lost tribe; it meant building a jungle house for Márcia and Suzuki to reach the Suruwahá; and it meant planting a church among those who had never heard—in short, it meant God's kingdom being advanced.

Instead I asked, "Are we in God's will, sweetheart?"

After a long pause Josephine said, "Yes. We are in God's will."

We hugged and pulled our three girls into an embrace, with Josephine reminding us, "Safer in God's will than anywhere else."

When I reentered the wheelhouse, small talk abruptly ceased. What I had done to Zezinho would have been humiliating for any man, and for many men from macho cultures, my words and actions would have cast me as a lifelong enemy.

"Zezinho, I'm sorry for what I said and did."

He immediately replied, "You're the captain."

"I had to take over, but the way I did—"

"Hey—you did the right thing. I'm sorry. I completely got it wrong."

Zezinho's humble confession immediately put us at ease. Soon, in an attempt to process our fears over yet another brush with death, we joked and laughed together. We knew the spiritual war wasn't finished, as the trip ahead of us was still long and arduous, but something changed in our hearts—and in the heavenly realm. The dark cloud of foreboding destruction that was hanging over us had dissipated. I also felt like I, and the *Abí* as well, had finally won the confidence of Ezekiel, Nivaldo, and Zezinho.

For the next day and a half we had a quiet trip. We went through a second shortcut that also had strong whirlpools, but everything went well. We traveled all night to the town of Tapauá, arriving at six in the morning on April 12. There we tied up next to a large public transport boat. Zezinho had planned to continue with us for a few more days, but when he heard the public transport boat was leaving for Manaus later in the day, he decided to return on that. We said good-bye to Zezinho and thanked him for his help as we transferred him and his stuff to the other boat.

THIRTY-TWO

Back to the Suruwahá

WE arrived around noon on April 18 into Caroço, the Ribeirinho community where Dave and Elizabeth were working. We were stunned to see everyone here since they were supposed to be building the jungle house by now. After docking, we found Jon and Denise.

"Why haven't you started building?" I asked.

Jon told us they'd arrived in Caroço about ten days earlier, stayed one night, then traveled another day upriver to Puma Bay. From there Márcia and Suzuki took them on a four-hour canoe trip on a small stream through thick jungle to the Baniwá tribe.

"We returned to Puma Bay the next day with Daniel, Fátima, and their two dogs. Everything was ready and we were set to go. In another twenty-four hours we would be at the Suruwahá trailhead unloading the boat and shuttling everyone to the building site."

Jon's tone grew heavier now.

"As we boarded Dave and Elizabeth's boat to leave, the engine wouldn't turn over. Dave determined the starter motor was dead. We were stranded there. A few days later a fishing boat came by. They couldn't tow us upstream to the Suruwahá trailhead so they towed us downstream, back to Caroço. Dave and Elizabeth's young disciple and deckhand, Kelky, hitched a ride with the same fishing boat all the way back to Manaus to get a new starter motor.

"Where are Suzuki and Márcia?" I asked.

"A river trader that Suzuki knew, named Zena, came through. Suzuki negotiated with him to use his empty boat hull for a month," Denise said. "They told him it would save him a lot of money in fuel not towing a big empty hull upstream. They also said that when he returned, our YWAM team would transfer the goods he acquired in trade from his main boat into the empty hull. He agreed. So we transferred the wood into the trader hull, and then Zena took Márcia and Suzuki to the Ribeirinho village nearest the Suruwahá trailhead."

After this update from Jon and Denise and a good night's sleep, we left early the next morning. Roberto, Jon and Denise, and Daniel and Fátima and their two dogs joined Ezekiel, Nivaldo, and our family on board. The *Abí* was overloaded, even without the wood for the house. The trip went well except that we had to fix the water pump belt that was wearing badly. We'd broken two already, and there were none to buy in Tapauá, so we had no spares.

Far up the Cunhuá River we passed a fishing boat traveling full speed downstream; obviously their freezer cargo hold was full of fish. We gave a friendly wave, like you do in these parts. As I did, a scripture verse came into my mind, "You do not have because you do not ask." I had learned over my nine years in YWAM that random thoughts are often God speaking.

My immediate thought was that we didn't have a fridge or a freezer to keep fish, but I still asked internally, "God, are you prompting me to buy a bunch of frozen fish for some reason?"

I did not have a strong endorsement in my spirit about buying fish. So I was dismissing the random thought as random, when the obvious suddenly splashed across my brain: *I need a water pump belt!*

"Nivaldo, take the wheel," I said.

I grabbed one of the broken belts from the engine room, hopped into the speedboat, and chased down the fishing boat. I needed a belt of a specific length, specific thickness, and a specific width, so the odds were a long shot. On a wing and a prayer I asked the captain, "Do you have a spare belt this size? I am happy to pay you for it."

The captain sent his mechanic to the engine room, and the man returned with two belts exactly like the one I needed. Keeping one for himself, the captain graciously gave me their second spare. Later that day the belt broke again, but, glory to God, we had a spare. It proved to me once again, and to the others on the boat, that God speaks and cares about the smallest details.

We were traveling into the night when just before bedtime a lone flashlight shone out of the jungle blackness, signaling us to stop. I turned our high-beam spotlight to shore, where an old man with a wrinkled, pained expression pleaded for help. We sensed it was important, so we stopped. Jon, Denise, Fátima, and Josephine got into a canoe and paddled to shore. Night sounds travel easily across the water, so I heard the elderly man ask if they could help his sick grandchild. I watched as the four of them followed the man up the muddy bank and into a simple hut.

After they came back, Jon and Denise described the smoky room where ten family members slept in hammocks. Sitting on the plank floor was a young mother holding a baby. Josephine, being both a nurse and experienced midwife, took over telling the story.

The mother told Josephine the baby was six months old, but it was barely larger than a newborn. Through a series of questions, she and Fátima learned that the mother had stopped breastfeeding soon after birth, in order to help with harvest. Since that time in December, she had been bottle-feeding the child lemongrass tea and feeding it thin rice porridge.

"So many of these families hidden in the jungle have no notion of good nutrition or the importance of breastfeeding," she said.

Josephine discovered they didn't understand, or believe in, the existence of microscopic germs; they thought the baby's sickness was a spiritual problem. The grandfather suggested it was a curse spoken against the family, while the mother suggested it was vengeful Catholic saints "getting back at her" for not being as devout as she should be. Because of these beliefs, the grandmother had invited a neighbor who practiced spiritism to ward off any curses through chanting over the child. For extra assurance, the spiritist brewed a special tea of jungle herbs and dead cockroaches and put it in the baby's bottle.

Fátima, shocked by the story, started reprimanding the mother. Josephine politely removed the bottle of witches' brew from the child and shared God's wisdom on nutrition and health care from books like Deuteronomy, Leviticus, Daniel, and Ezekiel. Then Josephine spoke of God's love for them. Fátima, Jon, and Denise prayed for the child and the family and bound demonic spirits. Josephine finished by leaving them with antibiotics to kill the germs that were causing the intestinal infection, no doubt saving the baby's life.

We arrived in Delícia, the Ribeirinho village nearest the Suruwahá trailhead, on April 22. This village did not have an outboard or long-tailed motor of any kind, so the wood was still in Zena's trading hull. It was too heavy and too far to paddle the wood in dugout canoes to the jungle building site, so Márcia and Suzuki had been waiting there for about a week.

The next morning, with fourteen on board, the *Abí* and the hull full of wood arrived at the trailhead on the Coxodoá stream. When I had visited four and a half years earlier, the inlet was only about ten feet wide and two feet deep. But that was dry season. Today the entrance was about 100 feet wide, with many feet of water over what used to be long, sloping banks. I drove the *Abí* in and nestled her in the mouth of the stream, just off the Cunhuá River. Densely grouped trees marked where the Coxodoá ended and where the thick jungle began. In spite of this distinct demarcation, the floodwater flowed right through the trees many miles in every direction. We tied up in the middle of this water world and turned the engine off. Everyone breathed a sigh of relief and gave thanks to God. The journey had been so full of difficulty. Even the long-term tribal missionaries said they had never before experienced such intense spiritual and physical battle.

We physically could not hold fourteen people to sleep out of the rain on the *Abí*, so everyone except Josephine and the girls went forty minutes upstream to where Suzuki and Márcia had decided to build the house. For the rest of the day we set up a jungle base camp. We erected a simple tarp roof for Daniel and Fátima and one for Roberto, Ezekiel, and Nivaldo, who would sleep under them in hammocks. They had two dogs and two guns for protection. My family, Jon and Denise, and Márcia and Suzuki would sleep on the *Abí* and travel back and forth each day in a canoe with a long-tail motor. We had just nineteen days to make a large clearing and build a jungle house, instead of the ninety days we had originally planned. I didn't know how we would do it.

THIRTY-THREE

Jungle Living

WE shuttled the timber to the stream's edge and cleared a space for building the house—two long and tiring days in brutal conditions.

"I hate to leave you and the girls on the boat all day, but it's not safe to go there yet."

Josephine shrugged. "Don't worry about us. We'll keep busy."

They certainly did. After cleaning up breakfast they sang songs, prayed, played music, and did arts and crafts and other preschool activities. Then they prepared food so it was ready for us when we arrived back in the evening. It was impossible for them to venture off the boat because the nearest dry ground was forty minutes away, where we were building the house. Josephine's local dressmaker had sewn loose long-sleeved tops and pants to protect the girls' fair skin from gnats and mosquitoes, but even so they couldn't go outside onto the roof or to the back of the boat because swarms of tiny black gnats attacked relentlessly.

At the building site, we hacked a clearing with machetes in one hand while waving away gnats with the other. The heat and humidity was smothering, yet none of us could wear shorts or short sleeves because any exposed flesh came under attack. Josephine sacrificed our spare mosquito net and sewed everyone a netted bag that we pulled over our hats and tucked down our shirts to protect our face and neck. Without this, even the short amount of time it took to hold a nail and hammer was insufferable.

We timed our arrival back to the boat at 5:45 each evening because that was when the gnats disappeared. Their departure sparked a flurry of activity as everyone hurried to wash clothes and do any outdoor dinner preparations, and then have a bucket bath or bathe in the river. Then as precisely as the gnats went off duty, the mosquitoes arrived in full force at 6:45. Only in that hour before dark did we have a chance to cool off.

Another frustration was that we caught very few fish, which we needed to supplement our rice, beans, and canned-food diet. "How come we're not catching fish?" Denise asked Suzuki.

"It's flood season. When the water goes over the riverbank, the fish swim off into the jungle in every direction."

Fishing by throw net in the jungle was impossible, and pole fishing yielded only a few small fish. We needed more protein, so each day somebody carried a shotgun should we see any wild game during our canoe trip up and back. One day I saw an eight-foot alligator sunning itself on a sand bank. I shot it right between the eyes, but it still dove beneath the surface.

"Did you miss it?" Jon asked.

"No. I hit it right in the forehead."

Suzuki turned the canoe around, and we searched for some minutes without finding it. "If you killed it, it will float to the surface tomorrow," he said.

Daniel, Suzuki, and I decided to hunt on land upon arrival. The floodwater concentrates the wild game into the high ground areas, making flood season the best time to hunt. The three of us, together with Fátima and the two dogs, set out. In less than ten minutes the dogs bolted into the jungle, baying loudly. Daniel, Suzuki, and I raced in pursuit, not knowing what we were after. Fifteen minutes later we found that the dogs had chased something down a hole.

"It's a wild pig," Daniel said.

"You can smell it," Suzuki added.

Sure enough, a pungent, oily musk smell hovered over the clay mound. Daniel and Suzuki cut branches into long stakes and pushed them through the clay, blocking the pig's exit. Daniel had learned this tactic from the Indians, who kill pigs with spears, he told us.

Daniel placed me at the front of the hole while he tied up the dogs. "Your 12-gauge will kill it with one shot. Are you ready?" he asked.

As I aimed my gun down the hole, Daniel and Suzuki pushed a long sharp stick into the back of the den. With a loud squeal the pig burst toward the exit but crashed into the sticks blocking its way. It fell with one clean shot to the head. Fátima sauntered up while we were field dressing the pig. Apparently she was keeping track of our location, which was good, because in the chase I'd lost all sense of direction. Suzuki and I carried the pig back to camp on a big pole between us. For the next two lunches and dinners everyone feasted.

The wood purchased in Manaus was sufficient for the floor, walls, doors, and windows, but we still had to source jungle material for a pole frame foundation. Daniel and Suzuki scouted out small hardwood trees, which we cut down with a chainsaw. We chose the five straightest trees for floor joists and cut ten other trees in half for twenty foundation posts. We carried these heavy timber posts on our heads or shoulders through the jungle back to camp, which was more than a mile away in many cases. After careful measuring, we dug deep holes and compacted heavy clay around the twenty posts into a perfect rectangle. Then we hammered the five floor joists horizontally on top of the posts, using huge eight-inch nails that were almost impossible to hammer into the hardwood. This took the entire first week, leaving only eleven days to finish.

"We're not going to get it done, are we, Jon?"

"Before I leave, everything will be done. No problem," Jon said.

The next day we laid the entire floor before lunch while Jon completed the measuring and cutting of framing studs for the walls. In the afternoon we framed the first external wall, attached the wallboards, lifted it into place, and nailed it down.

"See, I told you we would finish," Jon grinned. "Tomorrow we will complete the other three walls."

The next morning when we arrived, Nivaldo told us that when getting out of his hammock he saw a poisonous bushmaster snake within a few feet of where he was sleeping. He quietly reached for his shotgun and killed the snake.

"The gun blast startled us so much, we nearly fell out of our hammocks," Ezekiel said in his animated Portuguese. "But praise God he saw it before one of us stepped to the ground and was bitten."

That day we finished the external walls and began on the internal walls and the windows and doors. Jon worked with Márcia to build a sink area, kitchen counter, and some cupboards. Like the day before, Jon lifted the netting from his face each time he measured and cut with the circular saw; as a result he had hundreds of gnat bites.

The next morning Jon put a generous amount of insect repellent on his face in hopes of warding off the gnats. By the end of breakfast, however, his face was swollen and puffy—an allergic reaction to the repellent. Because Jon was also battling a head cold, Denise wanted him to have a day of rest. There were projects to be done on the boat, so I decided to stay back with him. This gave Josephine and the girls the opportunity to fit in the canoe and go to the building site in order to step foot on land for the first time in weeks.

Jon took the maximum number of allergy tablets to reduce the swelling and was soon fast asleep on the sofa. I didn't want to wake him with my banging in the engine room, so I decided to try my luck at hunting.

I glided into the watery jungle, paddling the speedboat upcurrent. Its wide hull protected me as I bumped against a paxiuba, a palm with black thorns six inches long. There is plenty of open space in the flooded jungle because not much sunlight reaches through. Tall trees with small leaves and choking vines with leaves the size of my paddle all climb high to capture the occasional glint of sunlight created by the breeze shaking the canopy. Wispy plants called epiphytes dangle from their towering host trees like streamers at a party.

I had heard monkeys close to the boat the evening before, so I scanned the treetops hoping they were still nearby. Besides the occasional splash of a fish jumping, the jungle was nearly silent. I paddled as soundlessly as I could. Monkeys have excellent hearing and eyesight, so they don't easily let you get close to them. I'd been paddling for twenty minutes when I spotted a troop of them munching on fruit. I stealthily guided the speedboat toward their tree. Three monkeys were near the top of the tree while three more were spread out on lower limbs. As I tied the boat to a small tree, the biggest monkey stood up and looked straight at me. I stood perfectly still for fifteen seconds while he literally looked me up and down. He had short dark brown fur over his body but a yellow and orange Mohawk crest that would have been the envy of the punk rockers I used to speak with in Hollywood. I couldn't help but grin as we stared each other down.

I was expecting him to let out a shriek to alert the others, but he started chewing again and sat back down. He obviously felt no threat as ample foliage stood between him and the barrel of my 12-gauge. One of the monkeys on the lower limbs, however, was exposed and within range. Since the chief did not warn the others, this one remained unaware of my presence. I slowly raised my shotgun.

Boom. The baritone blast rang through the forest. The monkeys bounded away in raucous leaps, free-running through the canopy. I continued to stare down the barrel of my shotgun. The monkey I shot didn't run, but neither had it fallen. I stared for a few more anxious moments until it fell with a loud splash into the water. I paddled toward the spot where I thought it went in but unfortunately the monkey didn't float like I'd seen waterfowl do when duck-hunting back home.

I had never considered what difficulty there would be in looking for a dead monkey under the water. I paddled back and forth, probing the bottom with my Minnesota ice-fishing spear. After a few unsuccessful passes I realized this wasn't going to work. The alternative was getting into the water and inspecting the bottom with my feet. By now the monkey had been bleeding out for more than five minutes. So who knew what the blood trail might attract—piranhas, alligators, and anacondas quickly came to mind. But I reminded myself that we hadn't had any meat or fish to eat since the jungle pig ten days ago. With my hunger spurring me on, I tied the boat to a small group of trees and jumped in fully clothed.

The water came right up to my chin. I walked forward, sweeping my feet out left and right across the bottom, using my four-prong spear to prevent being pushed backward by the current. After a few minutes I heard a loud splash. It set my heart racing. I was at least twenty feet from my speedboat. I hoped it was just a fish jumping, but if it was the splash of an alligator, I was dead. I remembered the alligator I'd shot last week. We never found it. Had it been stalking me? I was struggling to not let my fears get the best of me, when I kicked the dead monkey. My heart leapt. I speared the monkey and lifted it to the surface. It looked shocked, like it had been electrocuted. I did a fast slow-motion run through the water, pulling the monkey behind me until I got back to the safety of my speedboat.

Jon was awake at the *Abí* when I arrived home.

"Awesome," he exclaimed as I lifted the monkey from the boat. "I'm so looking forward to tonight's dinner. How long has it been since we've had meat?"

Jon's affirmation made me feel really good. Josephine was also pleased when she returned from the building site with the kids, giving me a big kiss for my hunting prowess. Fátima and Josephine talked excitedly about how to prepare the monkey, and soon the pressure cooker was spurting steam with the beautiful aroma of meat melding into Brazilian beans. When it was done, we were served a huge bowl of fluffy white rice and a thick stew of brown beans laced with shreds of monkey meat.

Fátima lifted a small bowl in her hands and said, "I know Kent shot the monkey, so he should probably be the recipient of this dish."

She looked at me as Josephine translated. I could see that Fátima was intending to honor Jon and Denise, so I nodded in agreement.

Having gained my permission, she continued. "Jon and Denise, you have worked hard and served with a happy disposition. The jungle house could not be built without your skills and leadership. To thank you, I have made this delicacy of monkey brains especially for you."

Jon and Denise both looked to me in hopes that this was a joke. Fátima put down the bowl in front of them, and Jon paled like he was going to faint on the spot. Daniel jumped up and grabbed the bowl. He immediately clarified that Jon and Denise did not have to eat monkey brains if they didn't want to. After some loving encouragement from Denise, and a few glasses of water, Jon recovered. Soon we were laughing and enjoying a marvelous meal of meat and beans over rice, while Fátima and Josephine sat out of sight from the rest of us eating the delicacy.

THIRTY-FOUR

Lábrea at Last

CONSTRUCTION was completed with a day to spare. Only the tedious process of making the thatch roof remained. Suzuki declared that to celebrate he would make açaí for us. Açaí palms lined the banks of the Coxodoá. For eighteen days up and back, we yearned out loud for the satisfying taste of the deep purple fruit pulp you could either drink or eat like a thick shake.

While the rest of the team built a raft on the stream's edge for washing clothes, I took Jon, Denise, and Suzuki in our speedboat to a stand of açaí trees. Suzuki, who'd grown up in a city near São Paulo, started scaling a forty-foot tree with a looped palm leaf tied around his bare feet to help grasp the trunk and a knife gripped tightly between his teeth.

"What are you doing, Suzuki?" Jon laughed.

"It's not dangerous. If he falls, he'll just fall into the water," I said.

Suzuki cut off the large panicle laden with fruit, then slowly slid down the trunk. We returned to base camp with six of these panicles, each holding over five hundred tiny fruits that looked like blueberries, only hard and black-purple. Suzuki put the thousands of berries into a tub to soak. The six panicles, now stripped of the berries, looked like and served as a bushy broom. Soon each of our Brazilian colleagues had one in their hands, sweeping the jungle clearing.

"Keeping it clear around the house keeps away the nasties," Márcia explained. "Snakes, small animals, even ants and mosquitoes don't like the exposure of a completely bare area."

After lunch Suzuki scrubbed the açaí berries on a corrugated washboard they had brought for laundry. He rubbed and rolled them to remove the hard outer shells and squeeze out the thin layer of pulp. By midafternoon Suzuki emerged triumphant, hoisting a two-quart plastic pitcher of syrup-like juice. Márcia called us together and ceremoniously handed each of us a cup and a spoon. Then, after expressing thanks to everyone for their hard work, she broke out her precious stores of sugar and pearl white tapioca that we mixed in as Suzuki poured each person a cup.

It was exquisite. The juice bars and ice cream trolleys in Manaus that offered açaí were always my favorite, but the freshly processed açaí was so delicious that we sat in silence savoring the complex, sensational flavors. Everyone finished with toothy smiles stained purple.

The next morning Jon and Denise loaded their belongings into Márcia and Suzuki's canoe. Sasha, Chloe, and Alexandra gave happy hugs while tears rolled down the cheeks of Denise and Josephine as they embraced. I gave Jon a manly bear hug.

"It's been awesome," Jon said.

"After the trauma I put you through, you say, 'It's been awesome'?"

"Hey, maybe once along the way I longed for home . . ."

"More than once for me," I said, and then we laughed together. "You know, Jon and Denise, practical servants like you, who do behind-the-scene projects, are so valuable. Missions just wouldn't succeed without you."

"Well, thank you," they both said.

"Take us as an example. Our ministry as a riverboat family would be sunk without you."

"Ha ha—very funny," Denise said, as Josephine rolled her eyes.

"I've been waiting to say that for six weeks," I said with a laugh.

We stood as a family on the back stairway waving off the tiny black gnats with one hand and waving good-bye to Jon and Denise with the other. Suzuki pull-started the motor and lowered the long-tail shaft into the Cunhuá River to propel them toward the Dení Indian village.

On May 13 the Wycliffe plane flew overhead and waved its wings, confirming the rendezvous had gone according to plan. The pilot then flew Jon and Denise over the Suruwahá village so they could see the maloca and the tribe they had indirectly served. There was an atmosphere of spiritual victory as the plane flew away. The atmosphere that had been so spiritually oppressive was now peaceful. God had won the victory! We sensed the heavens rejoicing with us over the completion of the jungle house.

The rest of us remained another ten days, collecting palm fronds to finish the thatch roof. Each large, round frond was folded in half and then nailed onto the roof poles, starting on the low overhang, going up toward the peak. On May 21 the roof was completed. Suzuki and Márcia rolled out a Home Sweet Home mat by the bottom step. The next day Ezekiel, Roberto, and Nivaldo and Daniel and Fátima broke camp and moved onto the *Abí* with us. We said good-bye to Suzuki and Márcia and prayed over them before they returned to their first home together.

The *Abí* engine had not started for a number of weeks because of an unknown problem. Assuming Dave and Elizabeth's boat was now fixed, Ezekiel and Nivaldo offered to go downriver in their canoe to request them to come and retrieve us. As they headed off, Josephine and I thanked Ezekiel and Nivaldo for serving us and sticking with us on the difficult maiden voyage. Roberto offered to stay with us and help navigate the boat to Lábrea.

The following morning, however, the river trader Zena, who owned the empty hull, arrived.

"Thank you again for the loan of the hull," I said and told of our success completing the house.

"Are you leaving now?"

"We would like to, but I haven't been able to start the engine for a few weeks."

"I could have a look at it, if you want."

"Oh, please do."

In thirty minutes he had the engine running. So only twenty-four hours after Ezekiel and Nivaldo left, we too started downriver. First we went to Puma Bay, where we helped Daniel and Fátima get back to their home. It took all day going up a small stream and then hiking through the jungle with our three girls, but it was great to visit the Baniwá village and see where they worked.

After that we returned to Caroço, arriving at dawn on May 27. We stayed the whole day so the kids could run and play on land with the village children. But the next day we said good-bye to Dave and Elizabeth and their young son, Joshua. They remained in Caroço, church planting in that Ribeirinho community.

On our second day out of Caroço we stopped to visit Paulo and Jorge's community development work in a Ribeirinho community near the junction of the Tapauá and Purus Rivers. I had been feeling weak, which I assumed was from the demands of hiking in and out of the Baniwá village, but when I began feeling worse, I went to see the nurse who worked with Paulo and Jorge. She was an American everyone called Gilli. She operated a small clinic and a malaria testing station. After drawing blood and looking under the microscope, she diagnosed me with the *P. vivax* type of malaria. She gave me chloroquine, the treatment of choice, saving us a three-day detour to the Tapauá hospital. By God's grace I mustered enough strength to speak in the small Ribeirinho fellowship that Paulo and Jorge had started.

We arrived in Lábrea, Amazonas, on Sunday, June 9. According to my log it had been seventy-seven days, and 277 hours in the *Abí*, since we'd left Manaus. Doing the math, I realized that 277 hours of driving is the equivalent of driving from New York to Los Angeles more than four times. Such are the distances in the Amazon. The marathon trip was done, but our long-term work among the River People was yet to begin.

PART SIX

A Family on a Riverboat

Jesus grew in wisdom and stature, and in favor with God and men.

LUKE 2:52

THIRTY-FIVE

Intercession Insights

W E were finally beginning our own ministry as a family on a riverboat; it seemed almost surreal. Our four and a half years in the Amazon had taught us that our spirits were most sensitive upon entry into a new place. Although Samauma was our destination, it lay within the Lábrea district. The governing municipality would certainly influence the hundreds of River People settlements within it. In prayer, the first thing Roberto, Josephine, and I sensed was that Lábrea had a strong indifference to spiritual things. We asked the Lord why.

"I get the impression of people coming to Lábrea in search of good health but falling prey to more sickness," Josephine shared.

Roberto replied, "Your picture is similar to what I wrote down: high hopes ending in shattered dreams; big projects resulting in wasted time and money; people with aspirations of success but ending in failure. Perhaps a deceiving spirit."

The next day we moved up to the Dutch mission. There I wrote detailed notes about our prayer time. What Roberto mentioned about a deceiving spirit seemed true; Jesus called Satan the father of lies in John 8:44. As I continued reading, John 10:10 made me realize that Satan's bigger objective is to steal, kill, and destroy. This caused me to recall the harsh vision of Isaiah 21—the first scripture I received about coming to the Amazon. I turned to that chapter again.

> "Rise up, captains, oil the shields," For thus the Lord says to me, "Go, station the lookout." . . . "I stand continually by day on the watchtower, and I am stationed every night at my guard post." . . . "Fallen, fallen is Babylon; And all the images of her gods are shattered on the ground."[5]

I had not understood what God was saying to me six years earlier, but it was clear now. God was instructing me that through prayer and intercession (station the lookout), and through spiritual warfare (rise up, captains, oil the shields), the destroyer himself would be destroyed.

So many hopes and dreams had been destroyed in the Amazon. I once read an article that pointed out that the two largest corporate losses of the twentieth century were both in the Brazilian Amazon. Henry Ford, the richest man in the world in 1927, bought a huge tract of land in an attempt to establish rubber tree plantations large enough to monopolize the rubber trade in the United States. He failed miserably.

Ford's losses, however, paled into insignificance compared to those suffered by the American shipping tycoon Daniel Ludwig, who was the world's richest man in the 1980s. He built an entire town and planted a vast tropical tree farm. His goal was to have one of the world's largest plantations and paper mills to supply the global demand for office paper. He, too, eventually abandoned all for a total loss.

After putting the girls to bed, Josephine and I reviewed the intercession notes and read John 10:10 and Isaiah 21 together.

"It cannot be a coincidence that the two largest corporate losses of the twentieth century were both in the Amazon," I said. "Both men were smart and the richest in the world, yet they failed at planting trees in the Amazon. It doesn't add up. All of this convinces me that the prince reigning over the principality of the Amazon is the spirit of destruction."

I sat in amazment at how God warned us, even before we came

to the Amazon, that the "destroyer was destroying." And destructive it was: the boat tipping over, the truck getting smashed, our stuff getting stolen, the bedroom burning up, the boat sinking, the engine catching on fire, losing the speedboat and Alexandra, then almost getting shipwrecked in the white water.

If the prince of the Amazon is the spirit of destruction, then who, or what, is the strong man of Lábrea? I set my heart on discerning this, pondering for a few hours.

Josephine closed her book and called out, "Come to bed, handsome man—it's late."

"Oh, how I wish I had understood Isaiah 21 six years ago," I lamented as I closed my Bible.

"Well, you can't do anything about the past," Josephine said, yawning.

"True, but we can do something about the future. Do you want to hear the future?"

"Only if it's short and fast," she said, closing her eyes.

"The harsh vision of Isaiah 21 ends with the promise that the destroyer himself will be destroyed. It happened before, in Babylon, so it can happen again in the Amazon!"

I flew to Porto Velho the next day to pick up supplies and take our belongings to Lábrea in our truck. I shared with Reinaldo and Bráulia the vision I had for our work among the Ribeirinhos, which I dubbed PAI, an acronym for *Posto de Assistência Integral* (Integral Assistance Post). Since many Ribeirinho communities had a school utilized only three hours a day for about half the year, my idea was to use a school building as a health post, church, and community center.

"I would call the multipurpose building *Casa do PAI*."

"Ooh, I like the vision," Reinaldo said encouragingly.

Of course they knew that *pai* is the Portuguese word for "father," so the building would be referred to as House of the Father.

"I really like the name," Bráulia said. "House of the Father is culturally relevant and it integrates community development into church planting, which I think is great."

John Dawson had said during his visit that one of the keys in breaking spiritual strongholds is moving in the opposite spirit. Certainly moving in the opposite spirit to the spirit of destruction is to engage in development. Planting churches through community development, therefore, resonated as the right spiritual strategy.

I shared the House of the Father vision with other staff that night, and then we had a powerful and moving time of prayer. Edmilton, a tall African Brazilian from Rio with a contagious smile and manner, confirmed that he would join us in Samauma in September. He would be our first team member, as Roberto would be returning home once I got back to Lábrea.

On June 21 at 4:30 a.m. I left Porto Velho in my truck, now packed to the gills. By five o'clock I was on the ferry, crossing the Madeira River back into the state of Amazonas. By 7:30 I'd traveled 130 miles, to where the paved highway turned east into a large town while the unpaved Transamazon Highway turned northwest for Lábrea, 130 miles away. I stopped at a truck stop to refill the tank with diesel.

"How long will it take me to get to Lábrea?" I asked the attendant filling my tank.

"The cargo trucks do it in about twelve hours," he said.

How could it take twelve hours to go only 130 miles? I thought. *I just did 130 miles in two and a half hours.* As I was thinking that, the attendant stopped filling the tank and looked me over intently, then my truck. Then he said, "But as for you, I couldn't say. I've never heard of anyone traveling the Transamazon alone."

That did not sound hopeful.

The Transamazon was everything I'd imagined it to be. The first ten miles was a series of farms and was obviously traveled regularly. I locked my hubs into four-wheel drive and did a fair share of slinging through mammoth mud holes hundreds of feet long. My winter driving skills were coming in handy. As the farms disappeared, so did the mud holes—and the road turned smooth. I completed the first thirty miles in only forty minutes. Just as I was thinking *This is going to be a piece of cake*, I came to the first of many river crossings.

It was a small river, by Amazon standards, with a wooden trestle bridge that looked like the ones that get blown up in Wild West films. There was a sizeable gap between where the dirt road finished and the wooden bridge began. Chunky planks resting on top of tree trunks spanned the gap. I had my doubts about how sturdy the bridge was, so I inspected it before driving on. Then, as I drove across, I had to move four big planks again and again, so my wheels would not drop through one of the many gaps. When I was finally across the bridge, I realized it had taken me forty minutes to travel four hundred feet.

There were almost a dozen rickety bridges and five rivers equipped with barges that I manually pulled myself across on. It took me precisely twelve hours to go those 130 miles. I had now traveled the Transamazon alone, but it was not something I wanted to do again.

THIRTY-SIX

Samauma

BACK in Lábrea throughout the next week, Roberto and I readied the boat and unloaded the truck's contents. Heavy-laden with bags, boxes, and cases like pack mules, we stepped gingerly down the muddy riverbank, then up the unsteady gangplank onto the *Abí*. Six years earlier Josephine and I asked God if I should go on the Amazon spy-out-the-land trip with Calvin and Todd. God had answered so dramatically by giving us the same verses from Mark 14:3–9. The day our boat sank, followed by that fearful maiden voyage, we needed those memories of God's divine guidance.

God's direction to us was threefold. First, we were to pioneer a YWAM base on the river in Manaus so that missionary riverboats could be harbored and maintained. Second, we were to support YWAM missionaries doing tribal work. And third, we were to church plant in unreached River People communites. Today, July 3, marked the beginning of the third step of this word from the Lord.

Having made the trip before, we knew that the journey upstream was about nine hours. Before untying and pushing out of Lábrea, we gathered as a family in the main room of the boat.

"Is everybody ready?" I shouted. "For adventure?"

"Adventure!" Sasha and Chloe shouted.

"Ad . . . wenter!" Alexandra said in a belated attempt to copy.

"It's just us—Daddy, Mummy, Sasha, Chloe, and Alex," Josephine explained in her Australian motherly tone. "You girls need to obey daddy and mummy exactly and immediately so that everybody keeps safe, OK?"

"Yes, mummy."

"Let's pray," I said, then we held hands.

Chloe prayed that the boat would not sink. Sasha prayed for her friends in Manaus. Alexandra prayed, "God . . . pray . . . have fun!"

"Amen," we all said together.

I started the engine and the girls giggled with delight and soon became silly with excitement. Alexandra was making faces and doing two-year-old antics, causing us to laugh. The boat felt spacious for the first time. I was the captain, navigator, and mechanic, and Josephine was the cook, deckhand, and first-aid officer. We were on our own as a family on a riverboat.

We thanked Roberto for his help and waved good-bye to him as we traveled out of Lábrea. Simple houses dotted both banks. The homes were rural huts with thatch roofs. Men stood in their canoes, fishing with round throw nets. Beans, cassava, corn, and other vegetables were planted on the bank nearby. Floodwaters had been receding since late April. The Purus River was again confined within its banks, so there was no danger of getting lost. As the river got lower, however, there was the danger of hitting a sand bar. This could knock off the propeller or the rudder. I did not have a depth finder, so I had to be cautious. The rule of thumb is to stay in the middle of the river going downstream, but when going upstream you travel in the shallowest water possible, which keeps the boat in the weakest current and saves you time and fuel.

We arrived late afternoon in Samauma—the destination we had been preparing for and specifically working toward for more than two years, ever since Senhor Pedro had invited us to come and provide health care to his community. After driving heavy poles into the thick clay and securing the boat, we walked up the bank and were exuberantly welcomed by Pedro and Isabel.

"God is good to have sent you," Pedro beamed.

"And we are thankful to be here! These are our daughters, Sasha, Chloe, and Alexandra."

"Do you remember our daughter, Gracie?" Isabel asked, turning to a young woman now twenty-five years old. As we entered their home we met their three youngest sons and were told that their three older sons were out fishing. Claudio, Adalcír, and João were now twenty-two, twenty, and eighteen respectively. The oldest son was married and lived in Lábrea.

We soon established our daily routine as a family. Each morning I did chores and cleaned the fish we had received that morning from Claudio while Josephine homeschooled in the main room. The energy and curiosity of our toddler, Alexandra, however, did not coexist peacefully with the studious dedication Sasha and Chloe had for learning the alphabet, and for learning math, which they often did by measuring out baking ingredients. Alexandra's eagerness to help Sasha and Chloe draw alligators, monkeys, and fish as decorations on their letters to be pinned up around the boat often resulted in exasperation. So I changed my routine and took Alexandra with me up to the community each morning. I sought to learn stories from the old folks and learn the Ribeirinho way of speaking.

Everyone loved Alexandra. Her chubby cheeks and funny demeanor were irresistible. If I was short on time or wanted to talk longer at a particular house, I would send Alexandra on ahead of me, accompanied by other children, to visit the rest of the houses. People would be upset with me if Alexandra did not pay them a visit each day.

"*Chegei*," Alexandra would yell—meaning "I've arrived"—accompanied by a hand clap to announce her entrance. Because the untreated river water was the source of much sickness, everyone knew that we did not permit Alex to drink water stored in their homes. But since the water to make coffee was boiled, she was allowed to drink the small Brazilian espresso shots called *cafezinho* at house after house. Making rounds in the community became her daily routine.

In late afternoon and early evening we went visiting as a whole family, being sure to reach out in friendship to all families. Our goal for the first six months was sociocultural belonging; in other words, to fit in and be accepted. The Bible says it like this: "The Word became flesh, and dwelt among us."

A book I read in my missions training said that Jesus became a Western-Aramaic-speaking, northern Galilean, blue-collar, religiously conservative Jewish male.[6] That was so complete and specific. I felt we needed to be specific like that if we were to be accepted by the Ribeirinhos and be effective in ministry.

Our strategy was to gain their trust by living among them, and living like them as much as possible. To this end we dressed like them, which meant we wore simple T-shirts and shorts. We also ate what they ate. They gave us fish every day, which was great, but it also meant if they went without fish one day, so did we. In exchange for this daily provision of fresh protein we gave them health care and development assistance. In short, we had an unwritten arrangement that they would give us what they could, and we would give them what we could.

After visiting the families, we returned to our boat before nightfall and took baths by drawing up a pail of water from the river. I would start the generator that gave light for reading or for playing games and for baking bread in a bread maker. We had a TV in the main room, instead of our bedroom upstairs, because we often used it for health care presentations. A couple of evenings each week we showed a Disney movie to the girls as a special treat. On movie nights the community children, and many adults as well, would hang onto the outside of our boat, peering through the windows to watch along. Come bedtime we had two fans in our bedroom, which helped us get off to sleep in the tropical heat. The generator ran out of fuel after about four hours.

The main room was our public space. Here we received visitors, and Josephine did health care consultations. On just our second day in Samauma, four very pregnant women packed into one canoe came to us on the boat. I helped each one waddle up the gangplank. They said how glad they were that we had arrived so Josephine could deliver their babies. Josephine looked shocked at the thought of four imminent deliveries. I knew she needed to examine these women, so I took the three girls with me in the canoe to collect our drinking water from the middle of the river.

"Bye, sweetheart. Have fun," I said as I paddled off with the girls.

"Pray for me. I need God's wisdom whether I should deliver their babies."

There was hardly time to pray, because the very next day one of the women went into labor. Being Josephine's first delivery in this community, it would build trust if it went well. And praise God it did; a healthy baby boy was born.

THIRTY-SEVEN

Divine Beginnings

THE next evening, a man named Pedro from the next community upriver, Estação, brought his fourteen-year-old daughter, Antonia, for a health consultation. She had congested sinuses, headache, and fever—a bad flu was the diagnosis. Because the juice from the cashew fruit is five times higher in vitamin C than an orange, Josephine prescribed cashew juice, water, and rest. Before they left, Josephine asked Pedro if we could lay hands on his daughter and pray for healing. He agreed, so we prayed.

The next morning I accompanied Josephine on a postnatal visit to the woman who gave birth the day after we arrived. As we climbed up the steep bank toward her house, Antonia appeared in the window.

"Look, it's Antonia," I said as she bounded down the bank beaming with health and a smile. "Antonia, God has healed you," I said looking her straight in the eye.

"I know," she replied.

"And only twelve hours after we prayed. That's a miracle!" Josephine declared.

Antonia returned a huge grin.

A few days later, shortly after midnight, we heard knocking on the side of the boat and a man calling for "Josefina."

His wife, Vanjira, had been in labor for a number of hours and needed Josephine's help. I got out the flashlight so she could see to get ready.

"Pray for me," Josephine requested. "I told Vanjira that she needed to go to the Lábrea hospital to give birth because of the risks, but she refuses to go."

Josephine gathered her midwifery bag, and then we walked down the stairs in the black of night. She got into a canoe with two men we had never seen before. I shot up prayers as she disappeared upstream toward Estação.

Josephine returned after breakfast. She looked too tired to talk, but I couldn't resist asking, "How did the delivery go?"

"Twenty minutes after I left, I noticed we were paddling right past the community—I could see candles and the glow of embers on the other side of the river."

"Where did you go?" I asked.

"We kept going upstream. I started to panic because I didn't know these men." Josephine's eyes got wider. "I was about to start asking questions when they turned to cross the river and paddled hard. The current carried the canoe right to the community. I was so relieved."

"Wow! That must have been scary. How did the birth go?"

"As I feared, Vanjira was only having weak and intermittent labor pains. Again I told her that a home delivery wasn't wise, but she was adamant and would not go to the hospital."

"So what did you do?"

"I invited her to pray, saying God could help her if we asked Him to. She readily agreed and we prayed right then, asking God for good, strong contractions and a trouble-free delivery."

"And?"

"Her light labor continued for a few hours, but very early this morning she suddenly got good, strong contractions and a healthy baby was born. Honestly, Vanjira was so malnourished and anemic and in such a weak state to give birth, but God's presence was tangibly with us."

On Saturday night, July 13, ten days after our arrival, we held a community meeting in the Samauma schoolhouse. We wanted to say who we were and what we were doing in their community. We explained that Senhor Pedro and Isabel had invited us. We honored them for their leadership and commitment to the community. As a nurse and midwife, Josephine's role was understood, and desired, by the community. Everyone clapped, even cheered for having a nurse in their midst.

My role, on the other hand, needed explanation. Men in River People communities fished, worked the fields, and pursued income-generating activities like collecting latex rubber, felling saleable trees, or cutting logs into timber. I knew I would not use my time in these activities. However, I also knew that a foreign Protestant missionary was a role they did not understand, or even want. So I told them that for the first few months I would be a learner, a trader, and a storyteller. Although I could never find a job in America or Australia as a learner, a trader, or a storyteller, these three roles exist in rural communities worldwide.

I began by saying I was a dumb gringo who needed to learn from them. This got a good laugh from the crowd, but also nods of agreement. "Even though I speak Portuguese," I said, "I want to master your way of speaking."

Ribeirinho communities spoke a much different Portuguese than what is spoken in Brazilian cities. They expect to be laughed at because of the way they speak. So learning their way of speaking would, I hoped, honor them and affirm their River People identity.

Besides learning their language, I said that I also wanted to learn about their families, their history, and the community. I said if the older generation could tell me stories, especially history, over a Brazilian espresso, that I would be most grateful.

Then I offered to exchange gasoline and some other things I had on the boat. I would exchange these things for services like helping build a house in the community, or help with laundry or the children. A riverboat trader is a common role, but one usually associated with exploitation. So I clarified I would only trade for the things or services we needed, and not for products to sell elsewhere. This avoided stepping on the toes of anyone already in business as a trader.

As for storytelling, I offered to tell Bible stories, and Josephine offered to give health care talks for women. In these parts, where most adults are illiterate, storytelling is an important educational and social activity.

After explaining my learner, trader, and storyteller roles, I could see I was understood and accepted. Everyone clapped again. After the meeting the women and children gathered around Josephine, while Pedro—Antonia's father—came straight to me and introduced Isaiah, the young community leader of Estação. Pedro and Isaiah said that, on behalf of the community of Estação, they were inviting us to work there too.

"Vanjira told my wife that Josephine is a very good midwife." Isaiah said. "And Pedro told me that his daughter was better the next morning after their visit. Both Samauma and Estação are small, so I am sure you can work both here and with us in Estação. Please come."

"I have already spoken with Isabel about telling Bible stories in Samauma on Sunday morning," I said. So how about we come to Estação and tell Bible stories on Wednesday night?"

Pedro bobbed his head up and down.

"That would be great," Isaiah confirmed.

Every Wednesday night for the next five months, most of the community would gather in the Estação schoolhouse. It had large holes in the floorboards and broken window shutters, and it was missing some roof sheeting, which made our meetings complicated when it was raining hard. We would teach some songs, which everyone seemed to enjoy, and then using the River People way of speaking I would tell a Bible story. Only the light of small diesel lamps illuminated the large colored pictures from our girls' homeschool curriculum that illustrated my story.

There was a hunger and respect for what we were bringing, and we were sensing God's favor. This is how a spiritual movement began to emerge.

THIRTY-EIGHT

Soccer and the Kingdom

W E fulfilled our social roles in the River People communities—Josephine as a nurse and midwife, and I as a learner, trader, and storyteller. Josephine expanded her role by training some people as health workers, while Senhor Pedro allocated me an area to build a small house for future team members to live. Building a little house proved to be an excellent way for me to engage with the men of Samauma. Behind this house Josephine and I planted a vegetable garden for ourselves, and also to use as a teaching tool on nutrition. We also planted a medicinal and herbal garden from the plants the Jarawara Indians gave us. These became a source of low-cost medicine that we used in health care.

Our first team member, Edmilton, arrived in September to assist us in ministry and to field-test a Gospel of John that Tribal Ministry linguists had paraphrased into the unique Ribeirinho Portuguese. The paraphrase drew even more people to hear the Bible stories I told on Sunday mornings and Wednesday nights. People loved hearing

Scripture stories in their way of speaking, and they began asking for their own copy, but since copying was expensive in Lábrea, we decided they should trade for it. Soon we were inundated with cantaloupes, corn on the cob, squash, a spiny cucumber vegetable called *maxixi*, okra, various tree fruits, loads of fish, and many watermelons. For about two weeks we received one watermelon in the morning and one in the afternoon, often with the name of one of our girls etched into the rind. The biggest watermelon was as long as our two-year-old Alexandra was tall, and just as heavy! It was harvest time, and members of both communities were sharing their abundance with us in order to own a photocopied Gospel of John. God was stirring their hearts.

One Sunday afternoon, after playing soccer in another community, I joined the guys from our combined Samauma-Estação team on the sideline to relax after the game. Several had gathered around Isaiah, the schoolteacher and community leader of Estação. Even though Claudio was the captain, they looked to Isaiah for leadership on the field. I thought this was because he was the best player, but people seemed to look up to him off the field as well.

After some small talk, Isaiah asked me, "So you can be a Christian and play soccer?"

"Of course you can. Why do you ask?"

"Visiting evangelists have preached that Christians can't smoke, drink, or play soccer."

"They said what? They said you can't play soccer?" I questioned in disbelief.

"I'd like to be a Christian, but those are the three things I do the most," Chico said.

Everyone laughed at Chico. Then Claudio interjected, "It's more than that. It's because Christians make a mess of our communities."

"What do you mean, make a mess?" I asked.

"The preachers give really good messages. And because we want to know God, we raise our hands for salvation—we all have." Everyone nodded in agreement. "But after we raise our hands, they divide the community between the Christians and the non-Christians and tell us not to associate with nonbelievers. Even if they're family."

"I'm sorry to hear that."

"In small communities like ours it's important for everybody to be friends and participate together in all social gatherings," Claudio concluded.

"Can't we do both?" I asked. "Like today for example, we had Sunday school this morning and played soccer this afternoon—isn't that OK?"

"No," everyone declared in unison.

"Why not?"

"Because of the bath," Chico said. "When the last preacher came through, we set fire to the dry grass upwind of the school where he was preaching and smoked 'em out."

Everybody laughed at Chico again.

"It's not because of the *bath*, Chico—it's the *Sabbath*," Isaiah corrected.

"What is that?" Chico asked.

"To Christians the Sabbath is Sunday. It means a day of rest," Isaiah explained. "The Sabbath is why we don't work in the fields but have our social gatherings on Sundays."

"But soccer is a social gathering, not work, so why is it a sin?" Chico asked.

Isaiah shrugged his shoulders and looked to me for an answer.

"Playing soccer is not a sin," I replied.

Some looked angry, some looked delighted, and most looked puzzled by my statement. I realized how confusing it must be to have different Christians emphasizing different doctrines.

"Since Jesus is the founder of the Christian faith, who is the most important person to listen to?" I asked.

"Jesus," everyone said.

"Let me tell you a story then."

The team moved in close to listen.

"One Sabbath Jesus was going through a field and his disciples picked some grain to eat because they were hungry. The religious leaders said they couldn't do that because picking grain was working. Jesus said they were not working but had picked some grain in order to eat. Who do you agree with? The religious leaders who said the disciples were working, or with Jesus who said the disciples were not working?"

"Jesus," they said.

"In the same way, I agree with Chico that soccer is not working."

"I can't believe I'm right!" Chico exclaimed. Everybody laughed again.

"Jesus said, 'The Sabbath was made for man, not man for the Sabbath.' This is why I said you can be a Christian and play soccer."

"OK, now I have a question for you," Chico said. "I am thinking of giving up smoking and drinking. It costs me a lot of money and everybody knows it is bad for you, but what about growing tobacco? It is half my income. How can I stop planting tobacco when the income feeds my wife and child?"

"Now that's a hard question, Chico. Let me think about that for a minute."

As the men waited for my response, I waited on God, asking for help. "God, please give me an answer," I pleaded in silent prayer.

Chico and the others waited, alternating between expressions of grave seriousness and a look of glee, like they had caught me with a question too difficult. I knew this conversation was significant, and I did not want to give the wrong answer. But the only thing that came to mind was not to answer Chico's question. I struggled with this, but nothing else came to me.

"I am not going to answer your question," I said.

Chico looked offended. Soon he stood up and turned to leave.

As he did, I suddenly knew what to say. "Why do you put me in the place of God, to tell you what to do, Chico?"

Chico turned around with a confused look.

"Can I provide for your wife and child if I tell you not to plant tobacco?"

Everyone went silent, and all eyes were on Chico.

"Do you believe that God has power to provide what you need, Chico?"

My question surprised him.

"Uh, yes."

"Do you believe that God can look after you, your wife, and your child?"

"Yes. I believe that," Chico said.

"Do you believe that if you ask God this question and He tells you, 'Don't plant tobacco,' that he will provide your needs in another way?"

Chico thought long and hard. Finally he said, "Yes. I believe he will."

Isaiah and Chico were quiet on the way home in the canoe. I knew God was working in their hearts. I was grateful for the YWAM culture that taught me to ask God about everything. This practice had prevented me from giving Chico a quick and uninspired answer, like I did so often in high school and college when I had wrongly assumed that my job description as a Christian was to give people answers rather than leave them thinking about questions.

In my missions training I discovered that Jesus directly answered only three of the 183 questions he was asked in the four Gospels. He mostly responded to people's questions with a story. Jesus's next most common response was to answer a question with a question. Yet a few times he didn't answer at all. I prayed that Isaiah, Chico, and the others would not look to me for answers but would rise to the challenge of seeking God for themselves.

THIRTY-NINE

Redemptive Love

BEFORE I chose missions as my career, I completed two years at university. Now I was beginning to feel a nudge in my spirit to finish my bachelor's degree.

"Why now, Lord?" I asked in prayer.

It seemed like terrible timing. We were settled in Samauma and many seemed open to the gospel. Spiritual momentum was rising in the community.

In my early years in YWAM, I completed three semesters of training schools and outreaches, so I inquired what it would take to complete my degree. A University of the Nations academic advisor informed me I needed an outreach, two independent studies that I could do anywhere, even while in the jungle, plus two more campus-based courses to complete the degree. Based on that news, we made plans that on our next furlough I would complete the two U of N campus-based courses that I needed in Kona, Hawaii.

After we made those plans, however, a significant complicating factor arose. Josephine was pregnant with our fourth child. Like with our first child, having a baby in America without health insurance sounded like foolishness instead of faith. But once again, God's guidance was contrary to conventional wisdom. For a second time we were to trust God by having our child in America without health insurance, and we were also to trust Him to do his work among the Ribeirinhos, even in our absence.

When we announced that we were leaving for many months, our friends looked obviously disappointed. They were convinced we would never come back. Schoolteachers, health workers, and preachers had come to Ribeirinho villages with promises to stay, only to leave after a few months of living in the unpleasant water world of the Amazon floodplain.

"Why are you going?" Claudio asked.

"We want to learn more about how to make Samauma a better place."

"Many have said they would come back, but we never saw them again," Claudio said sullenly.

"I promise we will return, Claudio."

"How do we know your promise will be any different from the others?" Claudio asked.

I was going to leave the *Abí* with the boatbuilder, so he could do some service he owed me. But as I stared into space thinking about what to do, I saw a misty rainbow in the sky from the recent afternoon shower. *He needs a sign*—that was the idea that popped into my head.

"As a visible sign of my promise, Claudio, I would like to leave our boat with you until we return."

To me, it seemed like a lot of work and responsibility, but the pledge seemed to instantly dispel his discouragement.

"So can you help me by looking after the boat? I can give you something in trade for doing so," I said.

"We will help, and I will ask the others about what to ask for in trade."

After a community meeting they requested I bring back a FIFA-approved soccer ball for the community in exchange for caring for the boat during our absence.

In November we left the interior and returned to Lábrea. Then we drove our truck on the Transamazon Highway to Porto Velho. Cargo trucks had used the road steadily since it had reopened in June, in a race to supply Lábrea with enough of everything to last through the wet season. Now the rains had begun, and the road would be closed soon. Heavy trucks had cut deep tire depressions in the clay road that the rains had filled with mud. The conditions created a four-wheel-drive heaven that was fun for the first fifteen minutes but not for the fifteen hours it took us to travel 130 miles. We likely would have spent a long night in the jungle inside our truck were it not for Edmilton. Numerous times our mud-covered coworker used shovels, planks, and pushes from behind to free the truck from the muck.

Christmas was fun and festive with Grandpa and Grandma and all the cousins in wintry Minnesota. In January we arrived at the University of the Nations campus in balmy, tropical Hawaii. It was heaven on earth for us. On our second night we joined hundreds of Christian staff and students at the community meeting held in a large open-air pavilion. We were in a tropical paradise without dangers, gnats, or mosquitoes; we could hardly believe the pleasantness.

For six months the worship and fellowship with colleagues was divine, and the teaching was inspired and relevant. I did the Leadership Training School and then the Community Development School. In both courses I did my projects on our missionary work among the Ribeirinhos. We received so much, even more than our capacity to contain it all. Our girls flourished in the creative learning environment of the Montessori school and preschool. Josephine attended health care and leadership training classes whenever she could, loving every minute of it.

On the last day of my first course, Josephine went into labor. Sometime after midnight our son was born in Kelakekua Hospital. We named him Jonathan Christian. In the excitement and drama of the delivery we did not pay attention to the exact time of the birth. So when the birth certificate arrived in the mail, I noted the date and time was March 25 at 12:55 a.m. I suddenly remembered that last year it was March 25 when the boat sank. I opened up a time zone converter that confirmed what I was suspecting: 12:55 a.m. Hawaii time is 6:55 a.m. Amazonas time. In other words, our son Jonathan Christian was born on March 25, exactly one year—to the minute—after the boat sank. This was such a specific demonstration of God's redemptive love that we felt overwhelmed with emotion. Only God could bring us from the worst moment in our life to such joy in just one year!

After that semester in Hawaii we returned to the Tribal Ministries base in Porto Velho.

"Welcome home!" Edmilton shouted as he threw his arms around us. Our whole family loved having Edmilton as our coworker.

After helping lead a three-month Community Development School in Porto Velho, we finally returned to Lábrea and the River People communities. Edmilton joined us, accompanied by six community development students doing outreach under my supervision. Our small team of three adults had now become nine adults.

Even after being away for a year, we believed God for breakthrough and a year of fruitfulness. No one would have guessed that breakthrough would begin through an elderly Irishman.

FORTY

Maçiarí

I WAS walking through the Lábrea plaza when a friend stopped me with a shout. "Hey, Kaio! Have you heard that Frederick Orr is here and is speaking at our church tonight?"

"Who is he?" I asked.

"Fred was one of the first Protestant missionaries in the region. He started our church, other churches too, plus a school and a seminary. You should come!"

"We'd love to come. Thank you for letting me know."

Having the chance to hear one of the first missionaries to Lábrea was an opportunity Josephine and I did not want to miss. That night, we squeezed into the hot and crowded church and hung on every word the elderly pastor spoke.

"In 1954, my beloved wife of five years, Ina, and I were sent out by the Acre Gospel Mission. We set sail from Belfast, Ireland, on a steamship bound for Brazil in order to help plant an evangelical church in the territory of Acre."

Frederick went on to explain that after the long voyage across the Atlantic and a journey up the Amazon to Manaus, they boarded a local steamship for Acre. Only halfway to their destination, tragedy struck. Ina became seriously ill and, within a day, died on board. The captain stopped at the next town so there could be a proper burial. Frederick carried the body of his twenty-nine-year-old Ina down the gangplank into town—the town was Lábrea. It was June 4, 1954.

The townsfolk quickly heard what had happened, so there was a large crowd of curious onlookers gathered by the time Pastor Orr officiated his wife's burial service. Although Frederick spoke only English, their faces showed that they understood his pain. The brokenhearted young man then left his bride in the Catholic cemetery of Lábrea and reboarded the same boat to the territory of Acre, where he achieved his goal of helping to plant a church.

Josephine's heart welled up with compassion after hearing this tragic story. After the service, we hurried to the front to meet the elderly pastor. There he told us something even more astonishing. He discovered later that everyone at his wife's burial heard the English that came out of his mouth as perfect Portuguese in their ears! The realization of this second-chapter-of-Acts miracle eventually led Pastor Orr to Lábrea, where he started a church and a school and lived for more than twenty years. We felt so honored to meet him. But his story triggered something in me that made me eager to get home; I was having a revelation about the "strong man" of Lábrea, and I wanted to confirm my insights.

I raced home and found John Dawson's book, *Taking Our Cities for God*. This book is about the power of prayer and how to break spiritual strongholds. I turned to the list of questions in chapter 8 about researching a city's history, and question 10 caught my attention: "What names have been used to label the city, and what are their meanings?"[7]

This question caused me to remember that I actually had a book about Amazon names. I had never read it because it was such hard work for me to read a technical book in Portuguese. It belonged to Zezinho, but he forgot to take it after he had helped us on the *Abi*'s fateful maiden voyage. It had stayed with me ever since.

The book was called *Topônimos Amazonenses*. Inside, it said that a toponym refers to a place name, especially one derived from a topographical attribute. Lábrea's original name had to do with a topo-graphical element, so it was featured in one of the book's chapters.[8]

The chapter on Lábrea explained that long before the Portuguese explorer Colonel Lábre had arrived and humbly named the place after himself, the original name was Maçiarí, a Puru-Puru word. The Purus River is named after these original indigenous inhabitants. Actually Maçiarí comes from two Puru-Puru words: *maçi* is a topographical description that means "the space between the bank and the jungle." This is translated as "high ground" because it refers to the areas not reached by floodwaters. The second word, *ari*, means, "to collapse out of the motive of weakness, sickness, or death."[9]

It's no wonder that Colonel Lábre found not one indigenous per-son living here when he arrived in 1871, because to them it was the high ground of the collapsing sick or falling dead. The conclusion seemed irrefutable: just like destruction is the prince over the whole of the Amazon, Maçiarí is the strong man over the region of Lábrea.

Suddenly the wisdom of hindsight became blatantly obvious as facts and events began fitting together in my mind. The medical researchers at the Instituto de Medicina Tropical do Amazonas in Manaus were concerned when I said I had caught hepatitis in Lábrea, because med-ical records showed a certain mysterious sickness happened in Lábrea more than anywhere else, which is why they called it Lábrea Fever.

We also had noticed that the Ribeirinhos and residents of Lábrea viewed sickness as normal living, whereas good health should be the norm. The local saying "Every family has a leper" indicated that leprosy was expected, because every extended family had someone with leprosy. What used to be an isolated leper colony of just a few was now an entire district. The rate of infection was one in one hundred people, whereas the national statistic for Brazil was one in ten thousand people. This meant leprosy in Lábrea was one hundred times the national average. Lábrea was statistically one of the worst places in Brazil for sickness, in line with the character of the strong man, the spirit of falling sick.

Missionaries, especially medical missionaries, represent a genuine threat to the strong man; therefore, he tries to "steal, kill, or destroy" them even before they arrive. This must be why Ina Orr fell sick and died as soon as the boat entered the territory under the authority of

Maçiarí. It would also explain why our twin baby died in utero, immediately following our first visit to Lábrea. And it explains why sickness
in Lábrea thwarted my second visit back to Samauma, tempting us to
contemplate leaving Brazil altogether.

John Dawson had told us in Manaus that breaking spiritual strongholds is done through directed prayer and acting in the opposite spirit.
The application of this would mean that health care, normally thought
of as only humanitarian activity, is actually a key weapon of spiritual
warfare for Lábrea and the Ribeirinhos.

Months earlier, I had set my heart on discerning the local strong
man of Lábrea. God's provision came through many prayers, personal
experience, books in two languages, and the story of an elderly Irishman. Who would have guessed?

The discovery of Maçiarí changed everything for us. I shared my
findings at our next team meeting, and as a result we reorganized our
ministry strategy around community development and health care.
Community development moves in the opposite spirit to the principality of the Amazon, destruction, while health care moves in opposition
to the strong man of falling sick.

"Spiritual victory requires using spiritual weapons," Edmilton
wisely said. So we decided to engage the strong man by first confronting
him on the heavenly plane through prayer.

Second, we confronted the strong man in the earthly realm. God
gave us 1 John 3:8, "The reason the Son of God appeared was to destroy
the devil's work." After prayer and discussion our team started calling
out points faster than I could write them down:

"We need to work in health care . . . We need to acquire medicines
. . . We need to do health promotion and education in the schools."

Josephine felt she was to create a comprehensive training program
for rural health workers, while Margaret, a physiotherapist on our team,
said, "I feel that I'm to do physiotherapy with leprosy victims."

"Let's do them all!" I declared. The team enthusiastically agreed. "In
fact, I feel we are to teach and preach health in church and everywhere
we go."

After this meeting, the community development students and
I put together a health promotion seminar. We brought this to rural

communities up and down the river over the next two weeks. As part of the seminar, we also conducted a baseline health survey that included interviewing mothers and weighing children under three years old.

Then somebody on the team had the idea to do the same seminar and survey in town. The results were startling. Our health statistics showed that undernutrition in the rural villages affected one out of three children, whereas in town it affected two out of three. This fact was revolutionary. The entire population of Lábrea had always assumed it was the opposite. My previous social research had shown the main reason many families moved from the interior was based on the assumption that their children would be healthier in town. Our surveys showed that the children living in town were actually less healthy than those in the interior.

Over four months, our two-fronted attack through prayer and health work "bound the strong man," just as is described in Mark 3:27. This, in turn, enabled us to "plunder his house," which resulted in so much spiritual fruit. For example, Lábrea's municipal secretary of education became a Christian through our physiotherapist Margaret, who treated his uncle who had leprosy. Upriver in Estação, a women's health seminar led by Josephine turned into a time of asking for forgiveness and extending forgiveness to one another.

By destroying mental strongholds through directed prayer, community development, truth teaching and health care, we plundered Maçiarí and took spiritual dominion. The harsh vision of Isaiah 21 ended with the destroyer himself being shattered on the ground. It had happened before, in Babylon, and it was happening once again, this time in Lábrea, Amazonas.

FORTY-ONE

Isaiah

MISSION work is not only destroying the mental strong-holds propagated by the evil one, it also includes building new mindsets and new structures needed to occupy the house over the long term. A church is one of these structures. The key to effective church planting is to identify and cultivate future church leaders. Over these months our team was continually drawn to Isaiah, the leader of Estação. He had heard gospel storytelling for about two years now, but he still wasn't a professing Christian. Our team strategy was to have more interaction with Isaiah, who, we sensed through prayer, was a true leader.

As our community development students widened their outreach, we discovered that many Ribeirinhos had a skewed understanding of what it meant to be a Christian. Some had been baptized as infants by Catholic priests, but had made no further commitment to the church. Some thought they needed to "clean up"—quit drinking, gambling, or having sex, or give money to the church—before God would accept them. Even Carlos, who I considered my most faithful disciple, a loving and kind man who exhibited the fruit of the Holy Spirit, shocked me with a belief he'd shared a year earlier.

When I asked if he was a Christian, he said, "Nah, I can't be."

"What do you mean, you can't be?" I asked.

"'Cause I don't know how to read."

I assured him that faith in Christ didn't require reading. But I did mention that reading the Bible would help his faith grow stronger.

Our students expanded into teaching adult literacy classes in both Estação and Samauma, and I continued storytelling on Wednesday nights in the schoolhouse of Estação. One night, while telling the story of the woman at the well from John chapter 4, I did not say the exact number of husbands the woman had been divorced from. Carlos shouted from the back, "She had five husbands!"

Afterward, I asked Carlos how he knew the exact number of husbands. He shared that during the year we were away, he had made his wife, Iraçema, read him a chapter every night at bedtime. I quickly calculated that they had read the photocopied Gospel more than fifteen times.

"That's amazing, Carlos! Keep it up."

The next day in Estação, I went door to door and asked everyone a hypothetical question: "If everybody were Christians, who would be the best pastor?"

The results were unanimous: Isaiah. I found this result remarkable. Even José and Azusa, who were Isaiah's older siblings, recognized his leadership qualities. It also confirmed what we had sensed in prayer as a team. Because so many in Estação were supportive, even though there were only three Christians, and because many who attended the women's health seminar repented and experienced forgiveness, Josephine and I felt there was sufficient spiritual and social momentum to start a church. So on that Saturday morning before we left Estação to return to Samauma, I spoke with the three Christians, Azusa, José, and Pedro.

"Do you think it's time to start a church here in Estação?" I asked.

"Oh yes, absolutely," they agreed. "People are ready."

"So, when are you going to do it?" I asked.

"Us?" they questioned in disbelief.

"We thought you would do it," José said.

"Isn't it your job?" Pedro asked.

"It's your community," I replied. "If you want a church, then you have to start it. So think about it, and pray about it."

They looked at me in shock. "OK," they said soberly.

"I'll see you Wednesday night," I said.

Back in Samauma on Monday, I heard that Estação had had a church service the night before. I wasn't expecting that. I was surprised that Azusa, José, and Pedro had acted so quickly, literally the next day. I knew the first service would be really important, so I was a bit nervous and anxious to hear how it went.

Arriving back in Estação on Wednesday, I went straight to Azusa's house and asked her to tell me about it.

"After you left on Saturday, we went door-to-door inviting everyone to come Sunday night to the schoolhouse for a church service."

"That was fast," I said.

"Well, why not?" she asked innocently.

"You're right, why not?!"

"Everyone asked who was comin'," Azusa continued. "'Nobody,' I told 'em. 'Just me, José, and Pedro.' That got a chuckle out of most, but they all came, even more than Wednesday night to hear you, Mr. Kaio. I think everyone was curious—you know—to see how we'd do it."

"How did you do it?" I asked.

"Well, José thanked everybody for comin' then opened with a prayer. Next, Pedro got about half of his ten kids up there to lead some worship songs. I had to preach, 'cause neither José or Pedro know how to read, and don't know much of the Bible either. Then José thanked everybody for comin' and finished with a prayer. That was about it."

"How do you think it went?"

"When it was done, everybody clapped."

"Sounds like you did great," I affirmed.

"But we'll do better this Sunday," Azusa assured. "We had a prayer meeting here last night, and Pedro's kids are having worship practice tomorrow night. And we thought we'd do Sunday school like you do in Samauma, on Sunday mornin' for the kids."

"Wow, four meetings a week—after only the first week! Keep up the good work, Azusa. I look forward to hearing your report next week."

Over the next seven weeks Azusa, José, and Pedro faithfully led Sunday school in the mornings and a service in the evening. During these weeks, just as Josephine anticipated, about six women declared their faith in Christ, including Chico's wife and Eliete, João's wife, from Samauma. The other four women, all from Estação, included Pedro's wife and their daughter Antonia, whose healing in the first week of our arrival had led Pedro to give his life to Christ.

The YWAM team and I intentionally stayed away on Sunday nights. The social movement and spiritual momentum seemed to be increasing rather than decreasing, even under the quiet leadership of Azusa, José, and Pedro. They were faithful deacons and wise elders, the perfect church council, you could say, but unfortunately they were not charismatic or in any way natural leaders. Losing momentum would be the death knell to the infant church. We needed a breakthrough and we needed it quickly.

It came eight weeks after the first church service. Edmilton and one of our team members, Helena, had helped with the Estação Sunday school that morning and stayed with Isaiah's wife, Joanna and their four children for the day while Isaiah was playing soccer. Once he was back home eating dinner, the worship songs began, kicking off the evening service. Isaiah hadn't finished eating, but jumping to his feet and wiping his mouth he said, "I have to make an announcement before church starts." Then he dashed off.

"Leave your plates. We'll do the dishes after church," Joanna said.

"Don't worry, Joanna. We can do them now," Edmilton and Helena volunteered.

"No, leave them. Isaiah wants us in the church service, including both of you," she said.

When they arrived, Isaiah was already up front speaking. He was talking about the three YWAM missionaries who worked with the Jarawara Indians: Beth, Sandra, and Afonso. He said they always scolded him for selling alcohol to the Jarawara.

"You know that with my teacher's wage I would buy things in town, including alcohol, and sell them up here to make a little extra money. That extra money helped provide a better life for my children than I had. But now, I've decided to stop selling alcohol. Not because Beth, Sandra, or Afonso told me to, but because God told me to."

Edmilton and Helena realized that Isaiah was making a public declaration of faith. He went on to share how his parents had become Christians after his older brother, José, was born. They named their next child, a daughter, Azusa after the revival in Los Angeles. Then they named him and his younger brothers, Joel and Elias, after Old Testament prophets. Yet because he loved to play soccer, Isaiah avoided church. Later he got baptized in the Catholic Church only so the priest would agree to marry him to Joanna. His story was long and complicated, but it was glorious.

Some thirty minutes later Isaiah concluded, "I have decided to become a Christian. For many years I've known it to be true, but in these last two years I've finally been able to see a way through. If you want to join me in following Christ, come up here right now."

Raimundo, Pedro's oldest son and the worship leader, put down his guitar and joined Isaiah. Immediately four more young men from the soccer team went forward, as did his wife, Joanna, with all four children in tow. Isaiah was about to lead the group in a salvation prayer when he said, "Wait, I haven't said the prayer yet myself." So he called over his brother and sister, José and Azusa, to lead them in a salvation prayer.

After that prayer Pedro stood up and addressed the church. "Missionary Kaio asked around some time back, and everybody in the community said that you, Isaiah, would be the best pastor. Problem was, you weren't a Christian yet. Because of that we had to start the church without you. But seeing as you're already the community leader, and now you're a Christian too, it only makes sense that you should be the leader of the church as well. José, Azusa, and I will be right with ya, but as church elders."

"That's right, little brother," José said.

"Excuse me, Pastor," Azusa said with a smile. "You interrupted worship."

"So I did. Raimundo, get your guitar," Isaiah commanded, "and let's praise Jesus!"

FORTY-TWO

House of the Father

T H E goal of every missionary should be the planting of a church led by local believers. That goal was coming into sight for these River People communities, but not without opposition.

The baptism and inauguration of the church in Estação was set for October 12. As the date approached, new resistance arose from Senhor Pedro and Isabel of Samauma, who prohibited their son Claudio from being baptized, when he requested their blessing to do so. They also told him that if Eliete got baptized, as she was intending, she would no longer be considered family.

"What should I do?" Eliete asked Josephine and me about Senhor Pedro's ultimatum.

Remembering my reply to Chico some months earlier, I said, "We can't tell you what to do. But do you believe that God can speak to you?"

"Yes," she replied.

"Well, that's all you need then," Josephine added. "And don't forget, 'God works all things for the good of those who love him.'"

Tears welled up in her big brown eyes as Josephine gave her a hug and prayed for her.

Josephine and I were stunned. We had served in Samauma for two years, but clearly our message hadn't moved their deeply rooted folk religion, at least not yet. Although the landowners of Samauma continued to be good hosts in exchange for health care, they made it clear that a formal expression of faith, such as baptism and an active church, was not welcome in their community.

Estação, on the other hand, did not experience such opposition, since a large number of the community leaders and their family members were now Christians. Pastor Isaiah's leadership gifts flourished, as did the church. Through his testimony, his younger brother Elias and his wife, Maria, came to faith in Christ. They were living in Jurucuá, where three students made a two-year commitment to pioneer a church through community development. Elias and Maria assisted our team in that community.

Also at this time, the YWAM community development team near Tapauá contacted me about Jorge and his new wife, Evi, joining our team. Since Claudio's brother Adalcír bought the house I had built in Samauma, we decided that Jorge and Evi would build another house. Thus they could continue plowing the hard spiritual ground in Samauma while providing ongoing training and support to Pastor Isaiah. Jorge was a Brazilian from the south but had many years of experience in the Amazon. His wife, Evi, was half Baniwá Indian and half Ribeirinho, so they fit the job description perfectly.

We decided that immediately after the baptism we would move off the boat and into the house in Lábrea we had purchased. This was so the community would know that Isaiah was truly the leader of the church.

However, he was the first to question this move. "Why must you go?"

"As long as I am nearby, some people will presume I am the leader and pressure me to intervene if you do something, or say something, they don't like."

"I didn't think of it that way, but I see the wisdom. Still, I wish you didn't have to go. We will miss you here."

"We will miss you too. But don't worry, Jorge and Evi are building a house in Samauma and will help you in your role as pastor. We too are not that far away. We feel our next step is to plant a church in Lábrea, so Ribeirinhos have a welcoming place when in town."

The River People did not feel comfortable in any of the churches in town for two simple reasons: the first was you had to have shoes and nice clothes; the second was that church buildings were constructed of brick and mortar. On principle, many Ribeirinhos would not enter a brick home, living by the motto that true Ribeirinhos live in wooden houses. So there was a genuine need for a timber church that allowed Ribeirinhos to come as they are, shoes or no shoes, nice clothes or not.

The day of the baptism finally arrived. Pastor Isaiah and the church council of Azusa, José, and Pedro decided to call their church House of the Father Estação. In a simple ceremony on a sandy beach of the Purus River I baptized Isaiah. I made it clear to everyone that I recognized him as the pastor. I prayed blessing and God's anointing on him to serve his community as pastor of the first House of the Father church. He and I then baptized his older brother and sister, José and Azusa, and then Pedro, declaring them to be church elders. Then I got out of the river, leaving those four, in two groups of two, to baptize the remaining twelve adults. Of the sixteen believers baptized that day, only one was from Samauma—Carlos. João's wife, Eliete, and Claudio observed and gave encouragement, but they did not get baptized.

As we left the beach that day, I smiled at Josephine and said, "This is our dream coming true—a church among a previously unchurched people, the Ribeirinhos.

"As we plant, and others water, God brings the growth," she added.

When I designed our brochure before coming to Brazil, I thought Isaiah 33:21 was a cool verse to use because it was so descriptive of the Amazon, "a place of broad rivers and streams." But more than describing a place, that verse also declared a promise: "There the majestic LORD will be for us" (NKJV). It was a promise that proved true; the Lord had been *for* us.

The unremarkable schoolhouse of Estação, crookedly perched on the riverbank, sat above the wake of our riverboat as we guided the *Abi* downstream toward Lábrea. The first House of the Father church wasn't a building; it was people who experienced new birth in Christ and were committed to obeying him. Josephine was with me in the wheelhouse, holding our son Christian, now one and a half years old, while Sasha, Chloe, and Alexandra were at the back of the boat, seven, six, and four years old respectively. We waved good-bye to the infant church, our team members, our community friends, and to life as a family on a riverboat.

"Ministry is what we leave in our wake as we follow Jesus."[10] That was the phrase that came to my mind as the long bend in the Purus River carried us out of sight. Seven years earlier during the Amazon Praise in Song concert, I announced our public ministry by pointing out the other verse on our brochure, "Ask of me, and I will make the nations your inheritance" (Psalm 2:8). Josephine and I asked God for an unchurched people group, and He gave us the Ribeirinhos on the Purus River in the Amazon.

FORTY-THREE

Making Disciples of All Nations

W E settled into Lábrea with a new mission—to launch a church for Ribeirinhos who had moved into this bustling trade city on the Purus. The population was over 30,000, but it still had the welcoming and pleasant feel of a country town. Everybody seemed to know everybody; well, at least everybody seemed to know us, the only foreigners in town. With good local schools available, we decided to supplement our English homeschooling by enrolling our girls in the Portuguese-speaking primary school.

Only three months after the Estação baptism a DTS team from Los Angeles did ten days of outreach in Lábrea. Their evangelism birthed House of the Father Lábrea. This small gathering of about twenty met in a simple wooden house on the YWAM property. Leading this church turned out to be a family affair. We used the Sunday school and storytelling format, as we had done in the interior. I led a men's group,

Josephine led a women's group, and a lovely new convert named Mari Stella led the children. Because she was so new in her faith, Josephine and I would often check in to see how she was doing.

"Look," Josephine said to me as she peeked into the children's class. "Mari Stella is supervising, but Sasha is teaching the older kids, and Chloe is teaching the younger kids. Ah, that's adorable."

The next year, on the first anniversary of the Estação church, Isaiah baptized fourteen more, including Carlos's wife, Iraçema, and Chico and his wife. This meant twenty-six of the thirty-two adults in Estação were baptized as well as four adults from Samauma. The year after that, House of the Father Jurucuá emerged through the work of community development students who had made a two-year commitment. About a dozen were baptized, including two capable pastors, Benedito and Adalto. Our YWAM team of missionaries grew to fifteen, as the whole community development team near Tapauá, led by Paulo, relocated to Lábrea and joined us.

Paulo and his wife, Eliete, took over from Jorge in training and assisting the House of the Father pastors. Josephine, and our new coworker Gilli, the same nurse who had diagnosed me with malaria a few years before, created a comprehensive health workers training program. Fourteen rural River People enrolled. They came to Lábrea one week per month over two years. The communities they lived in helped them in their training by feeding their families and looking after their crops while they were away. This program received official and financial support from the Municipality of Lábrea, the State of Amazonas, and the National Health Foundation. The spirit of falling sick was now truly destroyed.

During this time Pastor Isaiah went to Porto Velho and completed the YWAM Discipleship Training School. Upon his return we held the first DTS for Ribeirinhos. Isaiah, Jorge, and Evi led the training, assisted by the Jurucuá team—Ana, Sergio, and Daniel—who had left Jurucuá shortly after the baptism and inauguration of the church, just as we did, so that the church would stand on its own.

Benedito and Adalto copastored in Jurucuá with wisdom and leadership. House of the Father Jurucuá then sent out Adalto, his wife, and their children as missionaries to a nearby community, where his parents and siblings lived. We had not taught overtly about missions, but the model of sending and going was before their eyes and was resulting in a spontaneous expansion of churches.

During these three fruitful years in the Amazon, I completed the remaining courses I needed and received a bachelor's degree in Christian ministry from the University of the Nations. It had taken me more than ten years to finish, but never mind. In addition to the degree, I possessed skills in language and culture, biblical development, sociology, and church planting, not to mention an incredible ten years of experience that I wouldn't trade for anything else in the world.

Studying while doing missions work was very rewarding. It allowed me to discern the steps of a Christian development process that would genuinely benefit the whole community. Jurucuá and Estação experienced many social benefits from having vibrant churches functioning in their midst. This process did not "mess up" the River People communities like Claudio said other ministry approaches had done. Mentoring local leaders was a key element to this success. Without payment, or the pressure to achieve organizational goals imported from the outside, leaders like Isaiah, Benedito, and Adalto were not only sustaining their churches and local development initiatives; they were expanding them. It was a process that was catching on, like a social movement. There was no term that described this Christian development process, so I coined one: *developmentoring*.

By God's grace, and with perseverance, we accomplished the three goals we had set out to achieve: helping start YWAM Manaus, supporting Tribal Ministries, and planting a church where there had not been one before. Yet, the ultimate goal, to make disciples of all nations, still seemed beyond our efforts. That is, until one hot Sunday in July, in the community of Jurucuá, where we saw it before our very eyes.

It was the first anniversary of House of the Father Jurucuá. Ana, the team leader, assisted by Sergio and Daniel, were cooking when we arrived. Since missionaries had a reputation of being social killjoys, we had sought to change that perception by putting on a big feast and celebration, complete with a soccer match, for all major church events and special days in the Christian calendar.

We joined with almost two hundred people for the feast and fellowship, and then in the late afternoon, we gathered in the cool Purus River for another baptism. Over a hundred people were in the water or at its edge, hearing the marvelous testimonies of the twenty or so getting baptized. Pastors Isaiah, Benedito, and Adalto did the baptizing. Those getting baptized asked for a second person to accompany and pray for them. This honor was often granted to Ana, Sergio, and Daniel, or to Elias and Maria, in recognition of their evangelism and discipleship in their lives.

After the baptism, this big crowd gathered into the simple wooden church that fit only about half; the other half had to stand outside. The three River People pastors, Isaiah, Benedito, and Adalto, were sitting up front while Ana, Sergio, and Daniel, along with me, Josephine, and our children, plus Edmilton, Helena, Gilli, Paulo and Eliete, and Jorge and Evi were sitting toward the back. As they began to play worship melodies they had written, we looked at each other with big grins. It wasn't our style, but what did that matter? They were worshiping in the Ribeirinho country music style they so loved. And that was the beauty of the moment; they expressed their worship in a way that was as unique as they were. In fact, if we liked everything about a church we pioneered, then it probably meant we did a poor job, as it would be more of us than them. The House of the Father Church in Jurucuá was no more Ana, Sergio, and Daniel than the Estação church was Josephine and me. These were not our churches, or YWAM churches. These were Ribeirinho churches, led by their own pastors and elders, in their own communities, with their own resources.

Even though we had never led a service, or even preached a message in the churches that we started, we sensed a spiritual shift take place as Isaiah preached. He had the right word for this moment. Those standing outside chatting suddenly quieted as a holy hush fell. Isaiah preached powerfully under God's anointing, his words and manner seasoned with grace. I turned to Josephine and saw tears; some were rolling down my cheek too. We were overwhelmed with a sense of spiritual fulfillment, gratitude, and joy.

Then, as we were served communion by Benedito and Adalto, we had a strong awareness that, in the heavenly realm, a spiritual transaction was taking place. They had already been leading, but from this moment on we could sense that they were now spiritually responsible for this movement. All twelve YWAMers present sensed it. We did not become spiritually irrelevant, but in that instant, we somehow knew that the special grace God had granted us for this mission task was now upon the Ribeirinho church leaders. We were seeing before our very eyes that the apostles we had chosen and discipled were the ones carrying out the Great Commission and fulfilling the ultimate goal of making disciples of all nations, one community at a time.

Epilogue

AFTER twelve years in the Amazon we moved to Australia. Miraculously, God once again gave Josephine and me the same verse. It was Psalm 16:5–6: "LORD, you alone are my portion and my cup; you make my lot secure. The boundary lines have fallen for me in pleasant places; surely I have a delightful inheritance."

Lábrea was an adopted place for us, but for our children, it was home. They did not want to leave their home, their school, their much-loved friends, and their life as they knew it, yet our guidance was clear. Our children were twelve, eleven, nine, and six at the time of our move.

Years earlier, we had invested our Australian inheritance in the Amazon based on his word to us from Matthew 19:29, "Everyone who has left houses or brothers or sisters or father or mother or children or fields for my sake will receive a hundred times as much and will inherit eternal life." Nine months after moving back to Josephine's home city of Adelaide, South Australia, we received as a gift, a block of land in the beautiful suburb of Belair, valued at about four times the amount we had invested in Brazil. This bountiful provision enabled us to build a new house, which was beyond our wildest dreams. We moved into our new home on July 3, 2003, exactly twelve years to the day after we had first arrived in Samauma. It was home for our children until they grew up, and it is still where we live today.

In August 2014, Josephine and I made a return visit to Manaus, Porto Velho, and Lábrea. We were astounded at the multiplication of the Christian population in Manaus, which now has one of the highest Christian percentages of any city in Brazil. The night we arrived, we went to the annual Jesus March, where hundreds of thousands of people were on the street praising Jesus.

YWAM still operates from the riverfront properties in the three original locations of Manaus, Porto Velho, and Lábrea. Tribal Ministries trains, sends, and supports teams to do tribal work throughout the Amazon, while all three locations minister in Ribeirinho communities. In addition they all train and send Brazilians to the rest of the world as cross-cultural missionaries.

As our small plane landed in Lábrea, our hearts and minds flooded with memories. Walking the streets, we were greeted with great fondness. Even people who were strangers came and told of how God had touched their lives through House of the Father churches.

The House of the Father Church in Lábrea outgrew their wooden building on the YWAM property, so a new one was built. We were amazed to see that today House of the Father Lábrea is the largest church building in town, with about 225 attending Sunday services. This church continues to work with YWAM Lábrea in serving and supporting ministry to Purus River communities.

We made a trip upriver with our small team of Australians, Brazilians, and Americans, which included our first supporter, my sister Wanda, and our previous coworker, nurse Gilli. In Jurucuá, Pastor Benedito and his whole community greeted us with a special meal. The church has continued to grow under his anointed leadership. It is hard to believe that he was once a simple Amazonian Ribeirinho who dabbled in shamanistic magic.

The Estação church now meets in Samauma; that's right, Samauma. We had served in Samauma for over two years but never saw a church form because of its deeply rooted folk religion. Claudio and his wife, Juliana, became the community leaders and eventually got baptized with Senhor Pedro and Isabel's blessing. Today, all houses have tin roofs, instead of thatch; the whole community has an ordered and clean appearance; and a community generator provides electricity to all the houses, to a K–12 regional school, and to the church/community center. The classroom has a computer with a satellite link. Claudio's brother Adalcír still serves as the community health agent. Samauma is now a model community based on Luke 2:52, where every community member has the opportunity to develop in "wisdom and stature, and in favor with God and men."

Claudio is the pastor of the combined Samauma-Estação House of the Father church, as Pastor Isaiah and Joanna now live in Lábrea, as do Carlos and Iraçema. There are about fifty in attendance on Sunday nights and a large Sunday school in the morning. The night we visited, Claudio and Juliana killed a pig and threw a big feast. Believers from Samauma, Estação, Jurucuá, Capaçini (the church Adalto started), and three youth from the Jarawara village came. These youth are Christians because of the work initiated by Beth, Sandra, and Afonso. It was a marvelous celebration. Many spoke of years past, but we spoke of our joy in seeing them faithfully following God today. We rejoiced that the small seeds we had planted continue to bear much fruit.

Today Josephine and I continue as full-time YWAM missionaries. Our heart is to inspire, encourage, and train Christians in the assignment God has for their lives. For about half of the year we lead a University of the Nations Community Transformation and Development School at the invitation of YWAM bases in Mexico, Australia, and other countries in South and Southeast Asia.

We are home in South Australia the other half of the year working in our ministry, Life Together Development. I offer services in urban planning, social planning, and international development. I teach in DTS, community development, and missions courses on the topics of evangelism, spiritual warfare, missions, worldview, and cross-cultural and community development. Josephine teaches in these schools too, as well as the Counseling and Health Care Schools. In particular, she teaches and leads a prayer ministry methodology she developed called His Presence Healing and engages others in supernatural evangelism.

We spend as much time as we can with our four children, who live and work in Australia, and who, by the way, in spite of being unwilling at the time, are happy that we moved to South Australia. Having said that, all four children count themselves as blessed, and richer in many ways for having grown up on the rivers and in the jungles of the Amazon. When asked, "How has growing up in the Amazon benefited me?" Sasha replied:

How hasn't it benefited me? I know multiple languages, have [international] friends, knowledge of different cultures, and can tell stories of sinking boats and amazing grace. But none of this would have been "normal" for me had my parents done "normal" for them.

If faith without works is dead, we were very much alive. My cool cat parents mixed faith with courage, "forage" (ah, see what I did there), which is the act of searching for provisions of any kind, which, if you're considering being a missionary, you may have to do at some point . . . It's always a risk to leave your safe space, but every challenge was an opportunity to grow in favor, with God and man. And we did.

Sasha completed graduate studies and works as a provisional psychologist. Chloe has master's degrees in both international business and marketing and works for the global business consultancy KPMG. She bought her own home and got married in December 2015. Alexandra made it onto Australian Idol, has sung backup for an Aboriginal rapper, and continues to do creative things as a hair and beauty consultant, including among celebrities on the Great Barrier Reef. Christian has also worked on the Great Barrier Reef and surfed many of the best waves of Australia, North America, Central America, Asia, and Europe. He completed a bachelor's degree in marketing and works in this field.

As for our fellow Amazon coworkers (in the order mentioned in the book):

Gerson Ribeiro continues in his call to serve and pioneer. He is director of a large organization in the northeast of Brazil that works in the areas of education, literacy, and microcredit to poor families who want to start small businesses.

Todd Kunkler has a BA in business administration and today is part owner and vice president of Dreamline Aviation Private Jet Charter. Todd is active in a college-based fellowship. He and his wife, Nancy, live near the YWAM base in Los Angeles.

Calvin Conkey and his wife, Carol, are the founders and directors of Create International, a global YWAM ministry that produces media resources on unreached peoples. They travel globally based out of Chiang Mai, Thailand. Calvin has a master's of applied anthropology and Carol a master's of intercultural communication.

Alcír Cavalheiro and his wife, Lourdes, led YWAM Belém for some years. They still live in Belém, where he is a pastor of a church.

Reinaldo and Bráulia Ribeiro led YWAM Porto Velho and Tribal Ministries for twenty years and then served at the University of the Nations in Kona, Hawaii, for about seven years. Reinaldo works in Christian counseling and Bráulia in missions and linguistics. They presently live in New Haven, Connecticut, where Bráulia studies at Yale University.

Anabel de Souza started YWAM East Timor in 1998 and still leads that work.

Baia and **Edilberto**, the two smiling deckhands, both trained as missionary pilots. Baia married a Swiss woman and flies for a mission agency near Belém. Edilberto married an American and flies for a regional airline in Washington State.

Todd and Terry Owens remain dear friends. They live in Chanhassen, Minnesota, and are godparents to our third child, Alexandra.

Bruce Ferguson lives in an apartment for senior citizens in Sydney. He continues to be an angel for us and others by interceding for ministers and missionaries daily.

Mike and Celia Naughton remain dear friends. They live in Melbourne and are godparents to our second child, Chloe.

Dave and Elizabeth Warner ministered in the Amazon for twelve years and then joined Mercy Ships, working at the international operations center in Lindale, Texas.

Luke Huber, founder of Project Amazon, died in an ultra-light plane crash after visiting one of the many River People communities where Project Amazon had a church.

Daniel and Fátima Batistela worked among the Baniwá Indians until chief Bidú and others responded to the gospel. They started and lead YWAM Rio Branco, Acre and are associate pastors of a church.

Mario and Jaçiara Silva led YWAM Manaus for about twelve years and then led in the United States for about twelve years. Today they are back in Manaus pioneering churches in rural towns and communities up the Negro River with the Presbyterian Church of Brazil.

Ezekiel Roque married Bráulia's sister, Cibele, and they led a home to rescue and restore street children in the city of Porto Velho. Today

Ezekiel is a lawyer on the Human Rights Commission of the Bar Association of Brazil in the state of Rondonia.

Nivaldo Carvalho married Janecir, and for a few years they worked on the team among the Suruwahá. Then he trained as a pilot with Mission Aviation Fellowship Brazil and now serves as a missionary pilot based near Belém.

Suzuki and Márcia worked among the Suruwahá for more than ten years and adopted a Suruwahá girl named Hakani. They both have master's degrees in linguistics and are the creators of UniSkript (together with David Hamilton). They have served as researchers/lecturers at the University of the Nations in Kona, Hawaii, since 2010. They also founded a national campaign in Brazil against infanticide (www.atini. org), which culminated in the approval by Congress of a law to protect indigenous children from harmful practices like infanticide. Their story is told in the book *A Way Beyond Death* (YWAM Publishing).

Jon and Denise Lundberg moved from Minnesota to Idaho. Jon teaches vocational subjects and coaches sports at Weiser High School. Denise is a school counselor. They are active in church, community, and supporting Christian ministries and missionaries.

Dale Olson married his Brazilian love interest, Suzie. Dale is a builder, and they live in Minnesota.

Kelky Justino remained in Caroço, leading the church started by Dave and Elizabeth. Today Kelky works on a boat that travels between Manaus and Tapauá, where he and his wife, Lenice, live and remain active in their church.

Paulo and Eliete Gomes led YWAM Lábrea for eight years after we left before moving to YWAM in South Africa. Today they serve with YWAM in Swaziland.

Jorge and Evi pastored House of the Father Lábrea for a few years before moving to Jorge's home city in southern Brazil where he was ordained. Today they are pioneer pastors in arid and remote central Brazil but desire to return to the Amazon.

Brenda "Gilli" Gilfillen started and led a program for disadvantaged children in Lábrea for more than five years after we left Lábrea. She now ministers in a remote health and nutrition center among the Fula Muslims outside Gabu in eastern Guinea-Bissau, West Africa.

Edmilton de Sousa is an emergency medical technician with the fire department and a pastor at the church where he grew up, the Church of the Nazarene in Nilopolis, Rio de Janeiro. He married his coworker Helena mentioned in the book.

Ana Fonseca married Francisco Xavier. They served as missionaries for a short time in Africa. Today they live in Belém.

Sergio Lima married Joseane from Lábrea. They both work in YWAM Porto Velho.

Acknowledgments

W E want to express our deepest gratitude to our YWAM colleague and editor Scott Tompkins. Scott helped us the whole way through as a mentor and editor. Scott and Sandi even invited us into their Texas home, enabling us to live, work, and learn alongside them for three weeks.

A huge thanks to Tom Bragg, Ryan Davis, and others at YWAM Publishing for editing and behind-the-scenes work, and the whole team in Seattle for their commitment to seeing this book published.

To our Brazilian coworkers and other YWAM colleagues, far too many to name, who journeyed with us over the twelve years in Brazil and have become lifelong friends.

To our extended families in Adelaide, South Australia, and Fridley, Minnesota, who graciously released us to "Go" and warmly welcomed us upon our return visits. A special thanks to DeLois Truehl, Johanna Tanner, and Anthea Tonkin, who carefully kept all correspondence from the Amazon years.

To our supporting churches, Parkside Baptist and Redeemer Lutheran, who remained alongside us in prayer and financial support, and encouraged us with love, prayer, wisdom, and short-term teams.

Thank you all.

Notes

1. Elisabeth Elliot, *Through Gates of Splendour* (Bungay, UK: Hodder and Stoughton, 1957).

2. Isaiah 21:2–4 (NASB).

3. Paul Cho, *Prayer: Key to Revival* (Berkhamsted, UK: Word Books, 1985).

4. John Dawson, *Taking Our Cities for God* (Lake Mary, FL: Creation House, 1989), 154.

5. Isaiah 21:5–9 (NASB).

6. Günter Krällmann, *Mentoring for Mission* (Hong Kong: Jensco, 1992), 43–49.

7. Dawson, *Taking Our Cities for God*, 85.

8. Octaviano Mello, *Topônimos Amazonenses* (Manaus: Imprensa Oficial do Estado do Amazonas, 1986), 152–56.

9. Meinke Salzer and Shirley Chapman, *Dicionário Bilíngue nas Línguas Paumarí e Portuguesa* (Dallas: SIL, 2006), 285, 154.

10. Leighton Ford, *Jesus: The Transforming Leader*, The Jesus Library (London: Hodder and Stoughton, 1991), 129.

Negro River meeting the brown Amazon River, with Manaus

Suruwahá grandmother caring for grandchildren

Suruwahá boys with blow guns, bows, and arrows

Chartering the Wycliffe plane into Lábrea

The house we bought in Manaus

Ywam Amazon: Gerson second left, Braulia, Reinaldo, Daniel & Fatima middle

Kent and Josephine with Loren Cunningham, who missed the inauguration but came to Manaus three years later

Family with the truck needed for the Transamazon Highway

Dilapitated log cabin in Manaus

The YWAM base in Lábrea

Translating for an outreach as DTS students preached the gospel in Lábrea

Meal with Senhor Pedro and Isabel in their kitchen

Living on the boat in the River People village

Boat sunk March 25 at 6:55 a.m.

Repairing the boat after it sunk

Life on the boat

Happy couple through the tough times

Our girls playing at the Manaus base

House of the Father began here on the YWAM base and today is the biggest church in Lábrea

Kent and Pastor Isaias in front of the Estação church they were building

Jurucuá church service led by River People leaders

KENT AND JOSEPHINE TRUEHL planted churches through community development among the River People and helped pioneer three Youth With A Mission (YWAM) bases in the Brazilian Amazon.

Today as YWAM leaders they travel internationally, teaching seminars on discipleship, missions, development, leadership, personal transformation, and prayer ministry.

They can be contacted at kentandjosephine@gmail.com.

Life in Amazon floodplain

First baptism, with Kent and Isaias

Josephine baptizing a visiting New Zealand health-care intern